THANK
GOD IT'S
MONDAY(?)

Balancing Work and Faith
While Keeping Your Sense of Humor

TOM C. PETERSEN

NASHVILLE

NEW YORK • LONDON • MELBOURNE • VANCOUVER

THANK GOD IT'S MONDAY(?)

Balancing Work and Faith While Keeping Your Sense of Humor

Published in New York, New York, by Morgan James Publishing. Morgan James is a trademark of Morgan James, LLC. www.MorganJamesPublishing.com

Unless otherwise noted, Scripture verses are taken from *THE HOLY BIBLE, NEW INTERNATIONAL VERSION®, NIV®*, copyright © 1973, 1978, 1984, 2011 by Biblica, Inc.™ Used by permission. All rights reserved worldwide.

Scripture verses marked NASB are taken from the New American Standard Bible, copyright © 1960, 1962, 1963, 1968, 1971, 1972, 1973, 1975, 1977, 1995 by The Lockman Foundation, La Habra, Calif. All rights reserved.

Scripture verses marked NLT are taken from the Holy Bible, New Living Translation, copyright © 1996, 2004, 2015 by Tyndale House Foundation. Used by permission of Tyndale House Publishers, Inc., Carol Stream, Illinois 60188. All rights reserved.

Proudly distributed by Publishers Group West®

Morgan James BOGO™

A **FREE** ebook edition is available for you or a friend with the purchase of this print book.

CLEARLY SIGN YOUR NAME ABOVE

Instructions to claim your free ebook edition:
1. Visit MorganJamesBOGO.com
2. Sign your name CLEARLY in the space above
3. Complete the form and submit a photo of this entire page
4. You or your friend can download the ebook to your preferred device

ISBN 9781636982342 paperback
ISBN 9781636982359 ebook
Library of Congress Control Number:
2023938939

Cover and nterior Design by:
Chris Treccani
www.3dogcreative.net

Morgan James PUBLISHING

Builds

with... **Habitat for Humanity®** Peninsula and Greater Williamsburg

Morgan James is a proud partner of Habitat for Humanity Peninsula and Greater Williamsburg. Partners in building since 2006.

Get involved today! Visit: www.morgan-james-publishing.com/giving-back

To Cathy, who has encouraged me, showered me with amazing grace, and in the process made me a better person

CONTENTS

INTRODUCTION:
Navigating the Conflict

Several years ago, I was sitting across the conference room table from a colleague in our company's investor relations department. We were arguing about what to include in an executive's presentation to an industry trade group. I wanted the speech to focus on industry issues, and she wanted the executive to talk about the company's financial performance.

I was frustrated because I didn't think a trade group meeting was the right forum for that topic, but she wanted to tell our story anytime we had a captive audience. It was a somewhat silly argument since no one—including the executive—would remember the speech as soon as it left his mouth. But I felt my position was the more responsible, practical, and statesmanlike approach.

And I felt her position was wrong. And maybe stupid.

Tempers rose and volume rose. As we went on, the content of the "discussion" took a back seat to the need for each of us to get our way. Eventually (probably when others came to see what the yelling was about), we decided we were done. Our bosses could solve this problem. We both left the confrontation feeling angry and frustrated and thinking the worst of each other.

This could have just been another day at the office. But the day before, I had returned from a Christian men's conference all fired up in my faith. The great speakers, joyous music, and positive energy lifted me up. I was excited about the opportunity to get back to work to witness to people, share the gospel, and be a shining light for Jesus.

Now, less than twenty-four hours later, I seemed to be working hard to break an important relationship with a colleague.

I wondered in that moment if it were really possible to successfully live out my faith at work. Is it possible to be gracious and kind and loving and still meet the organization's objectives? Could I honestly be expected to love others when the others were wrong? And potentially stupid? (Can I really be a Christian if I think other people are wrong and stupid?)

In that moment, my answer was "no." The conflict between work and faith was just too big to bridge.

Difference Between Work and Faith

Consider the differences between these two perspectives. First, there's my Christian self. I try to follow the teachings of Jesus. I try to model humility, kindness, and compassion. I try to think about others before I think of myself. I try to be generous and buy a box of Thin Mints every time a Girl Scout parent/coworker asks. I try to live in a way that makes people say, "Wow, I want whatever he has!"

My Christian self sees work as a means to an end. Work is an opportunity to use the talents God provided me to serve others and give him glory. It's a mission field for sharing the Good News.

Ah, but the work/world view of life is very different. Work tells me that my success is measured by the world's standards: a bigger title, more money, and a better parking spot. Work tells me I should be selfish, because if I don't look out for number one, no one will. Sometimes subtly, sometimes not so subtly, the world tells me my job should dictate my very identity. The world says that my stature, my self-esteem, and my very being are based on how successful I am at work.

That's ridiculous, I know. My identity is in Christ Jesus. Paul says so in Romans 6, Ephesians 4, Colossians 3, and all over the place.

And yet.

And yet there are days when the refrain of work is so pressing, so insistent—so obnoxious—that it's hard to hold those thoughts at bay. There are days when I have a hard time pointing to anyone I helped (aside from myself). There are days when I wonder whether my carnal nature has built up the Kingdom or helped tear it down.

And so the conflict rages. While my faith focuses on Almighty God, work strives for the almighty dollar. While my faith tells me to think first of others, my work signals that only the selfish are promoted. While my faith tells me to walk humbly with my God, work tells me to take credit for all my good works (and maybe a few works that aren't mine). While my faith tells me relationships are the only thing I will take into the next world, my work demands that I focus on the task at hand and worry about people later, if at all.

Every day it's a battle, a struggle, a balancing act.

I know there are people who can do both faith and work really, really well. They can lead with integrity. They demonstrate Solomonic wisdom when faced with work problems. They bring people to Christ while exceeding this year's sales projections. I know they exist because John Maxwell describes them in his books.

But I am not one of those people. You won't find me in written up in Hebrews (or John Maxwell's books, for that matter) as a great paragon of faith. I'm more like Peter when he's accused of being a follower of Jesus; I fold.

See, my basic problem is that I'm weak. I'm a sinner. I'm selfish, self-centered, and self-absorbed. (I spend a lot of time thinking about myself, too.) I demonstrate it every day, even hourly. I hear a Sunday sermon on Jesus's message of love, and I'm yelling at my kids before we've left the church narthex. I anonymously give to a local charity, and then vow never to give again because my name didn't appear in the glossy donor appreciation brochure. Paul took the words right out of my mouth when he wrote, "For I do not do the good I want to do, but the evil I do not want to do—this I keep on doing" (Romans 7:19).

It's a challenge all the time, but it especially confronts and confounds me at work. I mean, how do you bring glory to God when you think your boss is a jerk? (Not that mine is, mind you . . . but I know other people who think their bosses are jerks.) How do you constantly speak blessings when the customer is yelling at you over the phone? How do you stay focused on the eternal when the boss says, "I need this yesterday!"

Desire to Do Both Well

This is a critical conundrum, because I want to live out my faith *and* do well at work. I believe that God can assign us to the workplace as our ministry field. If there's a need for Jesus in the world—and a place where faith can make a difference—it's at work.

So I get spun tighter and tighter, one foot in each world, trying to balance the two. And, because I'm weak and a sinner (see above), I keep falling short.

But the good news is that God knows our struggle to not only survive but thrive. He provides a powerful tool for navigating these dangerous waters.

What is this God-given miracle tool?

Laughter.

(You thought I was going to say "prayer," didn't you? That's one bookshelf over.)

People have different ways of getting through challenges. I like to laugh. My theory is that balancing work and faith can be stressful enough. You only add to your stress if you take the conflict too seriously. You have to admit, it's a bit foolish to get too serious about work in this world when your destiny resides in another. So see the humor in it and laugh.

For me, humor is also a universal, adjustable, portable "problem-put-er-in-perspective." It functions like Excalibur, allowing me to slay whichever dragon—the job, staff meetings, the boss's favor—wants to take over my life. I like the quote from Dr. Madan Kataria: "If laughter cannot solve your problems, it will definitely DISSOLVE your problems, so that you can think clearly [about] what to do about them." Proverbs 15:15 says, "But a cheerful heart has a continual feast."

Some people take cars too seriously. Some people take sports too seriously (you know who you are, with your Green Bay Packers green-and-gold sofa). Me, I take work too seriously. I want to do well because I'm a responsible guy who thinks doing my best brings glory to God. (And if I get promoted and receive a big jump in salary along the way, well, that's OK, too.) But if I let it, work would kick my faith in the shin and push it off the ledge.

Laughter helps make sure I don't take myself too seriously. I try really hard to pretend I'm perfect at work because I've been taught that the closer you get to perfection, the higher you go in an organization. But, given my performance history, you have to recognize that hoping my perfection will get me promoted is pretty delusional. And funny. Convincing others of your perfection is difficult—and exhausting—when you're covered in the sludge of your past mistakes. (And it's gotten even harder since the internet was discovered as a great way to chronicle those past mistakes.)

Laughter helps me keep things in perspective. Rather than buy into the stress at work, I try to find the humor in it. I marvel at the ridiculousness, the foolishness, and the folly of it, and before you know it, work is small again, and my faith gets enough sunlight to grow.

Remembering to Laugh

I wrote this book to remind myself to laugh. It's meant to help me process the dilemma of work and faith when they seem in conflict. It also reminds me that Jesus has saved us from the dire prospect of a life continually chasing our work. When you have a heavenly perspective, it is much easier to laugh at the world of work. To paraphrase Romans 8:28 a bit (I do that periodically, when I can't find a Scripture that says exactly what I want to say), "He makes all things work together for good, even work."

There's another benefit to laughing at work. It's most effective when it's a social activity. It's a way to bond with others and share the experience so relationships are strengthened. When I am laughing at work, and I cause other people to see the humor in work, I feel like I'm helping them find balance, too. Laughing together about something at work is a kind of evangelism—a way of sharing that there's much more to life than work.

I don't have the gift of encouragement. (My gifts seem to be more along the lines of greed, envy, sloth . . . or maybe that's another list.) But maybe sharing these observations will encourage you. There's a chance (albeit slim) that you may find a fresh perspective in these pages. I hope this book assures you that someone shares your struggles. Maybe you'll see your work in a new way.

The Example of Nehemiah

The prophet Nehemiah is my hero in this effort. He demonstrates how to focus on his faith when he's having a bad day at work. He feels a call to leave his full-time job serving the king to return home to repair the wall around Jerusalem, a project that no one else seems interested in completing. Once he gets there, he finds a broken wall of bricks and a big barrier of critics and naysayers. His enemies try all kinds of tactics and say all kinds of mean things to prevent him from completing his task. But Nehemiah doesn't back down. He responds to their challenges with a plan of action and a heartfelt prayer. "For all of them were trying to frighten us, thinking, 'They will become discouraged with the work and it will not be done.' But now, O God, strengthen my hands" (Nehemiah 6:9, NASB).

This is my prayer for you and for me. That we are strengthened. That we focus on doing our work for God's glory, not to glorify the company or the boss—or ourselves. And that we find joy in our work. We should be joyful because we share the divine knowledge that there is more to this world than work. And we should be joyful because the world so desperately needs men and women of faith—and humor—at work.

Be strong. Be encouraged. We're not alone in our struggle. We have Jesus, and we have one another. Together, they make even the annual performance review seem a lot less serious.

But now, O God, strengthen my hands.

Section 1:

147 SURPRISING WAYS WORK AND FAITH ARE DIFFERENT (YOU WON'T BELIEVE NUMBER 68!)

Once you realize that work and faith are different, you either need to quit one of them or come up with a plan to navigate the differences. These chapters are meant to help you do just that! (Navigate, not quit. If you quit either work or faith, then you really don't need this book. It would be a nice gesture if you regifted it.)

CHAPTER 1

The Amazing Identity-Changing Employment

A job is an amazing thing. It not only has the incredible ability to pay your mortgage and put your kids through college, it also can define who you are.

I've seen it time and again. After searching for their *raison d'etre* (which, I believe, is French for "excuse to get out of bed in the morning,") men and women embrace their jobs as the source of their identity. They not only do their jobs throughout the workday, but their jobs become them. So much so that I have a hard time separating the person from the job. In my company, for instance, Bob is more "Boss" than "Bob." Leslie in facilities is all about her seventeen-pound key ring, and I have to wonder if Sofia the coffee cop would cease to exist (physically, if not existentially) if someone actually made a fresh pot of coffee after emptying the previous pot. (Names have not been changed to shame the guilty.)

My former coworker Kevin took this to a new level. For his late model minivan, Kevin paid the State Department of Motor Vehicles an extra twenty-five dollars for a vanity license plate featuring our company's marketing tagline. (I do not know how he convinced the DMV to permit all the extra letters to spell out "BuyStufFromUs," but I believe payola was involved.) While I admire Kevin's company loyalty, I fear something more sinister is happening here. He could have put any number of sentiments on his personalized plate—UIGRAD, GOCUBS, IMALOSR—but he chose to express his identity by aligning with his work. Either that, or he believes that such blatant company boosterism will put him in line for the next promotion. (If that's the case, I'm bummed that I didn't think of it first.)

Measuring Self-Worth

There are certainly plenty of aspects of work that feed a person's identity and self-esteem. Salary comes to mind as the preeminent guide to worker—and, sometimes, self-perceived human—value. But the problem with a salary is that it's not a good external yardstick. Unless you tell them, other people don't know how much money you make (the painful Salary Memo Incident of 2014 notwithstanding). If other people don't know your salary, it's somewhat hard to gloat about it. And telling them borders on tacky. Well, OK, probably steps *way* over that line.

Of course, you can flaunt your salary with a little conspicuous consumption, but that's not foolproof, either. Now that every U.S. citizen is guaranteed at least seven credit cards and a line of credit accessible on their phone, buying stuff for the purposes of showing off is practically a citizenship requirement.

So, people look for more tangible indicators of their identity at work.

Measures of Success

I often see office workers turn to technology to confer status. In fact, in many ways it's an all-out technology arms race today. It can get ugly. One guy (they are always guys when it comes to technology one-upmanship) shows up at a meeting with the latest version of the newest phone. But it's only a matter of time before everyone else has the same thing. And since every phone (except for my aunt's rotary cell phone) can do more than all of NASA could just two years ago, the phone technology race is not a good gauge of status. (I did have one coworker who claimed his phone also functioned as photocopier, espresso machine, and electronic fish finder. Granted, it's a handy tool for those times when he is answering email and enjoying a coffee beverage in the canoe on the lake. But what if he needs to take a call before his espresso shot is done?)

In the old days (B.C.—Before Covid), a person's desk location was a key part of his or her identity. A corner office on the executive floor, of course, was the pinnacle. We lesser beings would jockey for prime locations on lower floors. For instance, cubicles near the exit were highly prized because they allow someone to leave without the boss seeing them. The least of us were just thrilled not to share a cubicle. But the trend to non-assigned workspaces or even working from home has made work locations less of an identity perk. (Although there is always the woman who finagled the right to work from home permanently and doesn't miss an opportunity to point that out on video calls.)

For those of us who do go to the office, parking spaces also say, "I have more value than you." One company for which I worked had a clear hierarchy of parking. Most of us parked in city lots located what felt like miles from the office. But some very special employees, based on rank, were conferred the privilege of parking *inside* the building. And there were ranks of stature within the Building Parkers. Most people parked in white placard spots, but directors and above got to park in purple placard spaces. The highest of the mighty actually had reserved purple placard spots. Oh, how we pined to be a Reserved Purple Placard Parker someday.

Of course, if you're looking to a parking space for status, you need to consider what you park there. For instance, my 1997 Ford Escort hatchback would besmirch the value of practically any parking space the company provides.

Judge a Person by the Title

Titles are also a great way for employees to register status. For some people, titles are infinitely more valuable than salary increases or bonus payouts, because everyone knows right away what your title is. And unlike sharing your salary when you meet someone for the first time, telling someone your title is socially acceptable. Why, it's practically impossible to do business without it! Why even use a name when you have a great title?

"Hi, I'm Tom. I don't believe we've met."

"Hello, I'm the Assistant Associate Director of Corporate Initiatives and Strategic Research Programs. You can call me Assistant Associate Director for short."

I admit that I have a weakness for titles. In fact, when I worked at an advertising agency, I eagerly accepted a promotion from Senior Account Executive to Senior Account Executive and *Assistant Vice President.* There was no salary increase, no office relocation (not even a placard parking space), but I didn't care. I was the Senior Account Executive and Assistant Vice President of a five-employee ad agency. I was a force to be reckoned with! I expected clients to be in awe and coworkers to speak in hushed tones when I entered a room. And I did detect a noticeable elevation in respect when it was my turn to empty the agency's trash cans every Wednesday.

Finding Our Identity in Christ

Here's where Scripture can provide guidance. It may be easy to think of the Bible as a bunch of old stories about people with unpronounceable names living in countries that no longer exist. But the wisdom contained there has real value today. It's incredible to me how helpful Scripture can be in sorting out my current real-life issues.

Paul has particular insight for us on the need to find our identity in Christ. For instance, in 1 Timothy 4, Paul reminds Timothy that Christians have put their hope, not in the things of the world, but in the living God. In Romans 12:2, Paul encourages the church to not conform to this world, but to be transformed by the renewing of their minds. He makes his most direct plea to define our identity in Christ when he tells the Colossian church: "For you have died and your life is hidden with Christ in God. When Christ, who is our life, is revealed, then you also will be revealed with Him in glory" (Colossians 3:3–4, NASB).

We need to avoid letting the novelties of this life distract us from eternity. Paul is challenging us not to let our parking space, salary, office location, or any other accoutrement of work define us. The opportunity to be revealed with Jesus Christ in glory should be a much more tantalizing opportunity for us.

It's good to be recognized for our good work and enjoy the benefits that come from serious labor. But don't let it become your identity. We have a much more lasting and beneficial way of defining ourselves.

Believe me, I learned this a long time ago. There's a reason I'm now an Assistant Senior Executive Communications Coordinator and Wednesday Waste Mitigation Associate.

CHAPTER 2:

When a Good Work Day
Can Be a Bad Faith Day

What does a good day at work look like to you?

Is it a day when everything goes right? When you are named Employee of the Year the same day you are named CEO? When it's both a Friday and payday?

Those all qualify as good days. And maybe your standards are a little lower than that. Maybe a good day is simply going to a job you like, with people you like, driving to work on a road you like. Or staying home and working in pajamas that you like. Whatever your good day is, celebrate it.

I should also acknowledge that some people, notably some super-positive Christian people, will respond that every day is a good day. They rejoice that they are children of God and that today is another day to rejoice in God's love and share the Good News with everyone they meet.

Good for them.

I am not one of those people.

I think you can have bad days. I also think you can have really bad days and days so dull and listless that you forget them before they conclude. But I also believe God wants us to have good days and gives us a lot of tools and blessings so we can enjoy as many good days as we can accumulate.

I have given this a great deal of thought (generally on days that are not good days). I have identified several factors that propel a day from a fine day to a good day or even a great day.

Factors of a Good Day

To start with, good days for me are fun. Now, fun is kind of a squishy term, and it certainly exists in the eye of the beholder. Some people think spreadsheets and reviewing driver logs is fun. Again, good for them. I am not that person. For me, fun generally means doing interesting, strategic activities with people who are fun. Planning the launch of a new product is way more fun than a budget review meeting. Brainstorming with a talented team on ways to crush the competition is fun to me. Trying to figure out if we can ever recover after the competition crushed us is not fun. Fun is generally accompanied by a sense of winning (and if someone else loses, well, the following chapter about bad days was written just for them).

Good days for me are also days that are productive. During productive days, I generate copious amounts of work product. It's even better if I am generating a really good work product. I love days when I'm writing like a fiend and the words that show up on the screen are so wise, compelling, and poetic that I can't help but tear up a bit. I experience an endorphin rush when I come up with a new way of doing something or achieving something that we've been seeking, and then other people think it's a good idea, too!

That is a very different feeling than what I feel when I am sitting in a budget meeting trying to figure out how the office supplies expense dipped in March but seemed to rebound in April, but it was still shy of the five-year average for March expenses, at least in years when we didn't have new product launches. Days filled with those kinds of meetings never reach the status of "productive" for me. Or fun.

Aligned with those factors, a good day for me is a day when I feel that I am using the talents God gave me to full effect. (Now based on what you have read so far, you can argue that my writing, speaking, and ability to strategically delete emails should not be characterized as talents. But the funny thing is that my employer provides a salary for me in exchange for doing those very things, ostensibly contributing to the organization's success. It's not for me to second guess them. It's their money.) But I also have those good days when I believe—truly, deeply—that I am doing good work, that I am delivering something that is useful to my employer, and that I am uniquely gifted and positioned to do it. I have the experience, the education, and the vision to do it, and it's a pretty good result, if I do say so myself. That's a good day.

In My Own Spotlight

And if I'm being embarrassingly honest, another factor that helps define a good day is one that is Me-Honoring. They are days when I both do good work and get credit and accolades for the work I did. People give me compliments that I have done something that is darn swell. It doesn't have to be anything huge, like single-handedly beating back a shareholder revolt or solving our overseas supply chain issues. It can be as small as coming up with a clever headline for a story in the company newsletter. All it takes is someone to note it and compliment me on it. And if they invite me to a luncheon to award me Employee of the Year and CEO, even better. I have such a longing for admiration that, when I get it, that makes a good day.

Of course, I'm not really proud of that. I should never admit in public that "Me-Honoring" is something that I enjoy. This is, by definition, not "God-honoring." It will lead someone to suspect I am human.

Taking Credit for a Good Day

To summarize, I think good days are good. I think God wants us to have good days. I think God sets us in places where we can have good days. But I also think there can be a downside to good days. Beyond the good feelings, we have to be careful that good days don't leave us with a strong sense of self-sufficiency.

Maybe this never happens to you. Maybe every time you have a good day, you immediately give God thanks and credit for what he has done to make it a good day. Unfortunately, once again, I am not that person. Instead, too often, if I have a good day, I am so busy enjoying it that I don't stop to think how it happened. I'm soaking up the sunshine and picking daisies and feeling groovy. And if I do reflect on how I got here, I generally have a sense that *I* made it happen. I look at how I used my talents, my education, my vision to achieve a result, and I celebrate that. Yay, good day for me!

But God knows that about me, and he cautioned against that strong sense of myself. He saw that story play out long before I showed up. It's as if Moses' words in Deuteronomy were written just for me:

You may say to yourself, "My power and the strength of my hands have produced this wealth for me." But remember the LORD your God, for it is he who gives you the ability to produce wealth, and so confirms his covenant, which he swore to your ancestors, as it is today. *(Deuteronomy 8:17–18)*

Ouch. In lucid moments, I'm both embarrassed that I do that, and even more embarrassed that I'm in such good company that God cautioned against it thousands of years ago. I take some solace knowing I'm part of a long line of people who perceive themselves to be self-sufficient.

Antidote to Self-Sufficiency

How do we prevent ourselves from climbing a pedestal of self-sufficiency? I think it starts with understanding the talents that make me think I can be self-sufficient. It's good to recognize what I do well, but I also need to see things in a broader context. First, I need to recognize that God is the source of those talents. Yes, I may have accumulated experiences and education that lead me to do good work. But if I analyze how I got there, I can see God's hand in putting me in touch with people, opening the doors of educational opportunities, and arranging conversations and situations that allowed me to grow in my skills and knowledge.

Second, I can develop a deep sense of gratitude for the talents and opportunities I have been given. We shouldn't downplay our talents; they are gifts and provide us with the ability to do great things. But we also need to make sure we don't worship our skills as the reason for our good fortune. Author Os Hillman cautions that our strengths sometimes cloud our ability to see God at work. "When we reach a level of excellence and performance in our

fields, it actually becomes an obstacle to seeing God's power manifest in our work," he writes. "What we naturally do well becomes
the object of our trust."[1] What achieves results is not so much our
talents, but the talent-giver.

Jesus drives home the point in John that we are not indepen-
dent but flourish only in him. "I am the vine; you are the branches.
If you remain in me and I in you, you will bear much fruit; apart
from me you can do nothing" (John 15:5).

Good days are pretty awesome. We should celebrate them
when we experience them. But we should also use them as an
opportunity for worship, not of our talents, but of the one who
makes them possible.

And, once again, at the risk of repeating myself, I, too often,
am not that person.

CHAPTER 3:

When a Bad Work Day
Can Be a Good Faith Day

Work for me is pretty much paradise. I have an influential position making important strategic decisions that are implemented without question by a staff of thousands. I am compensated at a level far above my contribution to the company with benefits and perks that allow me to take lots of extravagant vacations. I have a huge office with great art on the walls, and my boss brings me coffee every morning just the way I like it. I hardly have time to work every day as I spend so much time getting massages, judging employee pastry-baking contests, and traveling everywhere on the company jet.

I'm kidding, of course. The art on my walls is pedestrian, at best.

But I do have a pretty amazing job. I give God thanks that I get to do work I enjoy with some particularly great people. And, if I'm really being honest, I have to admit I am being compensated at a level way beyond what I deserve. I am certain that the company could find someone willing to fill out time sheets and attend meetings for much less than they are paying me.

But for having such a good gig, I still suffer from the common worker ailment. I sometimes have a bad day. And by "sometimes" I mean "way more often than I would like."

Scale of Dread

If you work, I'm guessing you sometimes have bad days, too. They can range from the unpleasant to the unendurable. I have developed a handy scale that I use to evaluate my bad days. You might have something similar.

At the low end, there is the Tier I, the Uncomfortable. These are days when things just don't go well. The alarm doesn't go off. You miss the carpool (and it's your turn to drive). Your supervisor finds more things wrong than right in that important report. The team you lead generates way more problems than solutions. Vendors ship the wrong parts, meetings last way too long, your computer won't connect to the VPN, and Paul wears that cologne that makes you gag.

Tier I Uncomfortable days cause you to sigh. A lot. They wear you down. But they are not fatal. You can generally recover with a night at home, maybe by watching a mindless movie and ignoring your family members, until it's time to go to bed. In these cases, I will periodically have the wherewithal to pray that tomorrow will be a better day. And I double-check to make sure the alarm goes off the next morning.

The next level of bad days I calculate is Tier II, the Unbearable. These days are worse. And they may actually last more than one day. They may involve major setbacks at work: customers leaving for a competitor, storm damage to company operations, regulatory or legal setbacks, and a key employee quitting to become a social media influencer. Or a shepherd. (Having a good employee quit is bad, but if he or she leaves to become a shepherd, it's hard not to see that as a rejection of not only the work, but maybe your leadership.)

Tier II Unbearable days can push you to extreme frustration, sadness, and resentment. (And sometimes you can even exhibit emotions that aren't helpful to the situation.) And it all feels justified at the time. After all, these days are bad.

But it can get worse. Those are the dreaded Tier III days I call Cataclysmic. These are the really bad ones. I save this category for losing a job, bankrupting a company, or going to jail. Tier III Cataclysmic days move from broken relationships or operational mistakes to really devastating effects on an organization or an industry. I hope and pray that you don't experience these days very often. Because, frankly, if you are experiencing them on a regular basis, I kind of have to think you'd be better off buying books from the prayer section, one shelf over.

Making Our Response

Given the frequency of bad days here on Earth, the key is how you respond. My response is hopefully tailored to the severity of the day. For instance, at the Tier I Uncomfortable stage, I'm still trying to manage through it. I'm frantically working to keep my fingers and toes in the holes in the dam because I think I can control things through sheer effort.

But I think it's also probably true that I overreact to a bad day, regardless of where it falls on the scale. I can treat even the most mundane as a Tier III Cataclysmic event, based on my self-view and mindset at the time. When a true Cataclysmic day occurs, even my best effort isn't going to prevent any dams from breaking. (Which shines the light on another problem I have—erroneously thinking I can fix things. Of course, that doesn't mean I don't try. I have earned quite the reputation for exhausting myself trying to solve issues way beyond my span of control. I was *this* close to getting my arms around Middle East peace before the pandemic hit. It was a darn shame.)

While I am trying to manage my response to a bad day, I invariably will be confronted with a well-meaning friend or family member who sees my desperation (namely because I make sure everyone knows, in a loud and declarative manner, that I'm having a bad day) and offers words of comfort. They say things like "Chin up," "Keep smiling," and "Stop wailing during the meeting." Despite their efforts, their words of consolation do not help.

Then there are my Christian friends who feel compelled to tell me that I should be turning to God during these times. Of course, I know that. Duh! It's almost as if they don't see my stubborn obstinance as a conscious choice. If I am having a bad day, my primary response is to throw a ginormous pity party. And it is perfectly fine if no one else attends. I certainly don't need companions in this endeavor. I can achieve prodigious amounts of wallowing all by myself.

If my Christian friends or colleagues are particularly motivated to salvage me, they will share Scripture. It's here that my defenses start breaking down. I mean, how do you stay head down in sadness and discouragement when someone takes the time to remind you of the biblical model for responding to bad days? The answer is, it's hard, but I still keep working to avoid changing behavior. However, there's nothing like hearing Acts 5:41 describing the apostles suffering flogging at the hands of the Sanhedrin because they would not renounce their faith. After a good flogging, Scripture tells us, "So they went on their way from the presence of the Council, rejoicing that they had been considered worthy to suffer shame for His name" (Acts 5:41, NASB).

I think it's safe to say that I fall pretty short of rejoicing when I have a Tier I Uncomfortable bad day, let alone a day that involves flogging.

My Response

But despite my desire to remain feeling sorry for myself, feeling trod upon and unappreciated during a bad day, I have to pick myself up and keep moving. I have responsibilities to colleagues, family, and God to keep the whining short and move on to more productive responses. And I am pleased to say that, despite my intention not to, I have learned a few things that help.

Yes, Scripture is one of them. And there are lots of verses that apply. Some of my favorites:

- "The righteous person may have many troubles, but the Lord delivers him from them all." (Psalm 34:19)
- "Call on me in the day of trouble; I will deliver you, and you will honor me." (Psalm 50:15)
- "Once more the humble will rejoice in the Lord; the needy will rejoice in the Holy One of Israel." (Isaiah 29:19)
- "Though the fig tree does not bud and there are no grapes on the vines, though the olive crop fails and the fields produce no food, though there are no sheep in the pen and no cattle in the stalls, yet I will rejoice in the Lord, I will

be joyful in God my Savior." (Habakkuk 3:17–18, NLT) [And you thought Habakkuk was a fly-over book . . .]

But the verse that I find most useful for coping with bad days comes from Jesus during his final days with his disciples as he tells them as plainly as he can what lies ahead. "I have told you these things, so that in me you may have peace. In this world, you will have trouble. But take heart! I have overcome the world" (John 16:33).

I have gone back to this Scripture time and again for a couple reasons. First, it is a clear and declarative statement that Jesus is bigger than any problems we face on earth. Of course, at the time of those cataclysmic days, I may not correctly calculate the "greater-than, less-than" equation, but that's why we need to be reminded of that reality.

Second—and here's where I get to feel like I can have a little control—it helps to reset my expectations. I am so often surprised by how my response to a bad thing is because I have unrealistic expectations. But it's hard for me to be surprised that there will be trouble in this world, when the man who knows this world from its inception tells me that I will have trouble in the world. If I fail to accept that, that's on me.

In addition to checking my expectations, I find it also helps to check my feelings. For instance, when I flash emotions at Beth's request for help, am I reacting to the request, or to the years of her unreasonable rejections of the serial comma? (That's a purely hypothetical example, of course.) If I can get just a bit of distance from my bad day, I see that the events may be neutral (the alarm failing to go off at 6:45 a.m. is not, in itself, a negative event), but it's how that event affects my feelings when I start sliding down a slippery slope to feeling sorry for myself. Just understanding that my feelings drive my responses gives me pause that maybe my slump isn't warranted. After all, I'm an enlightened child of the modern world. How could I be so weak that feelings dictate how I respond to an external event? *Pfft!*

Finally, I find that gaining perspective can powerfully diminish the impact of a bad day. One amazing benefit to getting older is that you experience more bad days. While that may not sound like something to celebrate, the more bad days you experience, the fewer that you find are truly cataclysmic. Time does provide the perspective that so dramatically reduces the impact of bad days that it's almost, kinda, maybe, providential.

I laughed out loud recently when I came across a memo I had written to myself following what I thought was a truly cataclysmic event early in my career. (The fact that I wrote a memo to myself gives you some idea of the self-flagellation happening at the time.) I had made a typo in a company earnings release in which I incorrectly referenced the previous quarter's results. At the time, it was a truly bad day. I had to explain to lawyers and executives and the investor relations team what the mistake was and how I managed to make it. I had to humble myself in ways that were, shall we say, unnatural for a particularly brilliant young PR phenom. I had full expectations of being told to pack up my things, accompany the security guard out the door, and register a Cataclysmic day.

But I survived. In fact, I went on to make literally thousands more mistakes over the course of my career. I'm almost a little proud to say many of them were much worse than that! Although that day felt like the lowest of low points, with perspective I see how—what I thought at the time was the end of my career—had faded from memory until I found some written evidence to remind me of the details of the day. As added confirmation that the event has so little impact today, the company that I worked for at the time is no longer in existence. (I had nothing to do with that, by the way. That was due to someone else's Cataclysmic day.)

God's Hand on the Wheel

Perspective during a bad day also gives me the opportunity to ask myself, "Where is God in all of this? What is God teaching me in this event, and how do I respond to it?" Asking these questions rushes me from feeling the pain of the here-and-now to considering the forever-and-ever. I don't love that I have to go through a bad day to learn and grow, but I do love the idea that the experiences of a bad day can contribute to making me more useful to God. Os Hillman writes in one of his *Today God Is First* devotions that days like this provide assurances that God will deliver us through them, but also will use the experience to prepare us for greater victories ahead.[2]

Again, it's not easy to see or feel that in the midst of troubles in this world, but the more I practice, the faster I can get there. (Kind of like my ability to snag a soft drink from the refrigerator, make a sandwich, and grab a bag of chips when the commercial break comes on. I have it down to a science.)

Bad days aren't fun. But if they can be useful, well, then I guess that's what we get in this world. I appreciated the words of a guest pastor at our church when he said we have to decide whether we will *go* through a bad day or *grow* through a bad day.

I marvel at another example of Paul and how he responds with resilience even when he is beaten in Lystra while trying to spread the gospel. His success in healing people and creating Christians caused the Jewish elders to react violently.

"They stoned Paul and dragged him outside the city, thinking he was dead. But after the disciples had gathered around him, he got up and went back into the city…" (Acts 14:19–20).

Go back into the city where you were beaten? Even after that bad day? That requires spiritual focus and holy power.

That, and someone probably told him, "Chin up."

CHAPTER 4:

Dodging Bad Spiritual Fruit in Business Meetings

I don't recall the meeting agenda, the location, the participants, or even when we met. But I viscerally remember how I felt.

We were in a big group meeting. Although I don't remember where the meeting was held, I do remember being sequestered in the room, like we were marooned miles from civilization. (It's highly unlikely that we held the meeting on Devil's Island, but I do recall a sense that shark-infested waters would be preferable to that agonizing gathering. So maybe . . .)

What is painfully etched in my memory is how much I did not want to be in that room. I clearly remember the torment I felt, listening to an executive obviate, pontificate, and perorate about inconsequential things. I'm sure we were all gathered there for some good reason, some higher business purpose, but all I remember is daydreaming of the hundreds of other places I'd rather be.

There is nothing like a business meeting to define an employee work group. In that confined space, with stale donuts and unspoken agendas, you learn a lot about your coworkers, your supervisors, and your employer. In fact, I think every job candidate should be required to sit through a prospective employers' staff meeting before deciding to join a company. If we did that, I'm guessing it would be even harder to fill vacancies in the work world.

Maybe it's just me, but I often find myself in bad business meetings. I had another frustrating meeting the other day. I was sitting there, trying to be helpful, trying to honor God in the midst of the meeting. But I could see it was a lost cause. The person who talked the longest dominated the meeting, got his way, and in the process alienated everyone in the room. Fortunately, I was able to source Proverbs to passive-aggressively process the session later that evening:

- "Wise people store up knowledge, but with the mouth of the foolish, ruin is at hand." (Proverbs 10:14, NASB)
- "The tongue of the wise makes knowledge pleasant, but the mouth of fools spouts foolishness." (Proverbs 15:2, NASB)
- "A fool does not delight in understanding, but only in revealing his own mind." (Proverbs 18:2, NASB)
- "Do not answer a fool according to his foolishness, or you will also be like him." (Proverbs 26:4, NASB)
- "Do you see a person wise in his own eyes? There is more hope for a fool than for him." (Proverbs 26:12, NASB)

(If you ever want to be snarky, and yet do it with an air of scriptural authority, I highly recommend inappropriately applying a Proverb or two. Godly wisdom combined with my bad attitude. Score!)

Bad Business Meeting Fruit

Perhaps I'm being naïve, but I'd like to think that business meetings could be an opportunity to come together around a common purpose to do good work. Instead of creating collaboration and momentum, I too often find that my business meetings are showcases for cluelessness, boredom, and poor oratory skills. (Sometimes people who aren't me act that way, too.)

Business meetings are inherently challenging. They are complicated and nuanced. Invariably, there is more unsaid in a meeting than is said. It's one thing to have a successful interaction one-on-one with another person. That requires a level of engagement, attention, and empathy that can be exhausting all on its own. But the situation is made geometrically more challenging with the various matrixed relationships that happen when a group gathers for a meeting. You must consider how Person A interacts with Person B, B with C, C with D, who didn't hire E when F got promoted, even though everyone knew that G had promised the job to A, who turned it down. And J is just a jerk.

Then there's the power dynamic. At its most basic, the power goes from the highest-level person in the room and stair-steps down to the lowest—from executive, to director, to manager, to individual contributors. Each one has to look up to understand whether or not to criticize the idea or smile and express mild statements of affirmation. But there are underlying power dynamics, too. There is likely a subject matter expert, who is the one person in the room who has the professional knowledge to solve the problem. The key is to get that smart person to engage enough so that his or her eye-rolling is kept to a minimum. Then there's the person who has a particularly close relationship with a powerful person who is not in the room but who can quash whatever the group decides. You must be very careful to get the connected person to agree with your point of view, or all your handcrafted PowerPoint slides will be for naught.

Meeting Roulette

Meetings come in all shapes and sizes. There are the meetings called to figure out who in the organization is going to do the work that needs to be done. There are meetings to provide "input" for decisions that have already been made (or that will be made by that powerful person not in the room). Everyone later will need to agree to the decision because, after all, there was "input." And there are meetings called to identify who will take the blame for an organizational failure. These are not fun meetings to attend. My advice is that if you get invited to one of these meetings, call in sick. If you aren't there, you may be assigned the blame anyway, but at least you won't have to endure the process of having the blame assigned to you.

As a manager, I scheduled and held regular meetings solely to make sure team members lifted their heads from their computer screens long enough to realize they had coworkers working on projects very similar to the ones on which they were working. In some cases, they were working on the *same* project. I called these meetings "staff meetings." "Staff" universally dreaded these meetings, despite my best efforts to make them "fun." Apparently not everyone thinks a Neil Diamond sing-along is a fun way to start a meeting.

Role Playing

Once you successfully navigate all of that, you then need to be on guard for people adopting one of the many personas that can subvert a meeting. These roles are so common that most everyone has experienced a meeting with one or more of them. There are certainly more than I've listed here, but these are the behaviors that always aggravate me.

The Late Arrival: Whether you're meeting in the conference room down the hall or on a video call, one person invariably will be late to the meeting. Sometimes it's unavoidable, but when the same person consistently saunters into the room or onto the screen five minutes after a meeting starts, you begin to get frustrated. The challenge is compounded by the meeting organizer agonizing over whether to start the meeting without the person, or make everyone wait, thereby punishing everyone else's good behavior and rewarding the late arrival. At this point, I usually try to do something "fun," usually to less-than-satisfactory results. (Again, Neil Diamond sing-alongs are not crowd pleasers.)

The Disengaged: In any meeting, at least one person is there physically but completely disengaged from the discussion. She is doodling on her notepad, scrolling on her phone or, if the meeting is a call, clearly typing during the discussion. At least one person is disengaged regardless of the size of the group, but it's especially noticeable if there are only two people in the meeting.

The Techno-Challenged: This behavior can manifest in many ways: the individual whose phone keeps dinging during the meeting, the person on the call who just keeps talking even though we're yelling that he's on mute, or the person who insists she can get the laptop to project her screen if we just give her another moment. The number of techno-challenged people in a meeting is directly proportional to the number of deep, dramatic sighs heard during the meeting.

The Agendaless: This person is compelled to call a meeting but doesn't really seem to know why. She apparently assumes it's enough to find an open time on people's calendars, schedule a room, and dedicate an hour (or more) to the meeting, but fails to define what the meeting is about. By not identifying the meeting purpose, she also can't be blamed that the meeting didn't meet its objective.

The Expander: This person's purpose is to make the meeting longer than necessary. He discusses topics to death, asks questions that already have been answered, or debates points that were decided two meetings ago. I have a colleague who derives some psychic energy by tossing out unrelated comments simply to generate debate, regardless of the meeting purpose (which we would have known had we had an agenda). I happen to think it is a stretch to debate Panamanian monetary policy when the meeting was called to plan the department holiday party.

The Fumer: This person refuses to talk during a business meeting, sitting there with arms folded, glaring at other people around the table or across the screens. Apparently, this person didn't get the donut of his choice, wasn't invited to be on the "core" team, or is just fed up with the boorish behaviors of his colleagues. In response, he percolates silently in the corner. (Although in my defense, when you see two or more of the behaviors listed above, I happen to think I'm justified in my frequent fuming.)

At its very worst, a bad meeting looks like the attributes that Paul lists as outcomes of our sinful nature in Galatians 5. The list reads like a business meeting gone wrong: quarreling, jealousy, outbursts of anger, selfish ambition, dissension, division, and envy. (I will skip over other attributes that Paul lists, like sexual immorality, sorcery, drunkenness, and wild parties. If those are outcomes of your business meetings, perhaps even having an agenda won't be much help.)

Spirit Walking to Cure the Meeting Blues

In those rare moments of recognizing my personal responsibility, I have to admit that I have a role to play in making meetings better. It may be fun or an emotional release to mock the participants or the meeting dynamics to work out my own frustrations. But I also know I'm not honoring God when I do that. Instead, I should be centered on God so I can contribute rather than criticize.

After Paul talks about the manifestations of our sinful nature in Galatians 5, he contrasts that with the fruit produced by walking by the Holy Spirit. And the fruits he lists in Galatians 5:22 sound like a heavenly business meeting: love, joy, peace, patience, kindness, goodness, faithfulness, gentleness, and self-control. That list would make any meeting worth attending.

So how do we get that? Paul admonishes the Galatians—and us—to reject the pettiness and selfishness of earthly lives and embrace the Holy Spirit's power to lead us. Since we have accepted Jesus Christ and the Spirit into our lives, we have been given the freedom to no longer be under the control of our desires of the flesh. Instead, we can focus on serving others. Paul says so earlier in the chapter:

> You, my brothers and sisters, were called to be free. But do not use your freedom to indulge the flesh; rather, serve one another humbly in love. For the entire law is fulfilled in keeping this one command: "Love your neighbor as your-

self." If you bite and devour each other, watch out or you will be destroyed by each other. *(Galatians 5:13–15)*

What does that look like in a business meeting? For starters, I think it means I need to offer a thick covering of grace for my colleagues. I should spend less time disparaging their behaviors or the role they play in a meeting and more time listening to their points of view and honoring their perspectives. If the conversation goes off track, I should do my part to bring it back rather than disengaging. If we follow Paul's advice and walk in the Spirit, we could generate the right kind of spiritual fruit in meetings: peace, joy, love, and—be still my heart—self-control. It sounds like a nice contrast to the fruits of the flesh, such as strife, jealousy, disputes, and dissensions.

Paul's final line in Galatians 5 cuts deep when I think about my response to meetings: "Let us not become conceited, provoking and envying each other" (Galatians 5:26). I should be less focused on magnifying the dysfunction and more focused on contributing to a solution. Not only would the meetings go better, but I would be honoring my coworkers in the process. That would be a very different tact for me to take, but it feels like the right approach.

I imagine it would also dramatically reduce the need for a Neil Diamond sing-along.

CHAPTER 5:

Staking Your Claim in the Promised Land

I f you have spent any time in the world of work, you can undoubtedly come up with your own specific list of the ways that your job is different than your faith. Every job is different and aligns with and deviates from our faith principles in different ways. If your coworkers are all selfless individuals who are generous and altruistic, and your organization's mission is to spread the Christian gospel, then I would think the differences between work and faith are easier to navigate. If your coworkers are all organized crime bosses or notorious international arms dealers, however, then it might be a bit more challenging chasm to cross. (I'm picturing an awkward moment, when the new guy suggests to the notorious international arms dealers that they have a team-build day handing out holiday gift bags at a nursing home.) Regardless, each of us must resolve how to successfully maneuver between those two worlds to make a difference in each one. It can be a challenge, regardless of where you work.

Genesis before Robert Heinlein

The phrase "stranger in a strange land" always comes to mind when I think of Christians plopped down in the secular work world (which, let's be honest, is something like a cross between the former Soviet politburo and *The Matrix*). We tend to give author Robert Heinlein credit for the phrase, from the title of his science fiction novel. But the title references Exodus 2:22, when Moses, who escaped from Egypt to live in Midian, named his son Gershom, "for he said, I have been a stranger in a strange land" (KJV).

In fact, the Old Testament has several examples of individuals who find themselves in unfamiliar surroundings, from Moses to Joseph and Daniel to Amos. It should give comfort to those of us who feel we may not belong in the place where we are. Sometimes that uncomfortable place is exactly where God desires us to be. It makes sense when you think about it. Although fellow members of our congregations may need evangelizing, it's a wise move to distribute Christians throughout the work world to represent the truth and light that is our faith. It may feel disorienting at times for those of us in those roles, but Scripture shows us that God has done it many times before.

Picking a Position

Once we recognize that our daily disorientation may be due to the differences between work and faith—and not the new carpet smell at work—we need to determine how to position our

Christian selves in the workplace. I have found examples of a few different approaches to try.

The simplest approach is the path of work and faith simply coexisting. I think of the exiles from Jerusalem who were taken away to Babylon. Prophets like Jeremiah told the Israelites it was fine to relocate, because they would be allowed to continue to live, worship, and pray there (I presume mostly praying for the day when they could return home). I took this approach early in my work life. I knew I should be more "Christian" at work, but I decided that at work, the foremost requirement was to do work according to the rules of work. Yes, it's a bummer we're in a strange land, but let's just go along to get along, whaddya say?

I also have seen people take this to the extreme of rigorously compartmentalizing work and faith. I can think of coworkers who I know are Christians, but they would never let others know that. They prefer to keep their two worlds separate. My friend Connie built an invisible wall so her work didn't interfere with her faith and her faith didn't spill over into her work. When a colleague once asked Connie for her Christmas plans, Connie coolly explained that she preferred not to share personal details of her life. That might have been awkward but understandable had she not just spent twenty minutes regaling everyone with details of her bunion surgery.

I see elements of the faith quarantine approach in Psalm 141, when David prays that God will keep him separate from fellowshipping with the ungodly so he doesn't become like them.

Set a guard over my mouth, LORD; keep watch over the door of my lips. Do not let my heart be drawn to what is evil so that I take part in wicked deeds along with those who are evildoers; do not let me eat their delicacies. *(Psalm 141:3–4)*

(I certainly understand the danger of hanging out with the ungodly, but I draw the line at not eating their delicacies. What if they bring cheesecake to the office? I'll associate with them just long enough to get my slice, especially if they also bring cherries. But after that I will totally avoid hanging out with them.)

Another way to position ourselves at work follows the example of the spies Moses sent to Canaan to scope it out before the Israelites move in (see Numbers 13). Joshua and Caleb come back from the trip all jazzed that this was a land of opportunity and prosperity. The prospects of milk, honey, and giant grape clusters made it worth any obstacles they might face. They were ready to conquer it. In today's work world, I'd equate it with fellow believers who get excited every day about the chance to live and work in the work world, boldly sharing the gospel to colleagues at every opportunity.

Of course, there is the danger of taking it too far, illustrated by those who are almost belligerent in sharing their faith and try to convert coworkers by force. (I'm thinking of the guy in my community who shows up at public events with a bullhorn, shouts of condemnation of sinners, and his handmade posters. Given how I react when someone confronts me at a public gathering place about my sin, I'm never convinced this is the most effective approach. But I also know I don't have a lot of room to talk when it comes to a conversion track record, so perhaps I'm not the best judge.)

Wearing My Vestments Under My Suit

Unfortunately, my approach isn't so bold. Rather than expressing the exuberance of Joshua and Caleb, I'm much more like the other spies Moses sent out. I'm freaking out that the Nephilim are giants, that the land will devour me, and the conference room cof-fee pot only has decaf. I'm intimidated and a bit frightened at the prospect of being noticed as a Christian at work. So I take more of a stealth approach. I try to lay out enough indicators that people can guess I'm a Christian, yet I make sure I don't ruffle any feath-ers in the process. I call this my "sleeper cell" operation. I'm posi-tioned and ready to act if I need to suddenly demonstrate faith, but I'm not too obvious that it makes anyone uncomfortable.

One technique to do that is put out knickknack indications of my faith. I have items in my office that, taken together, would lead someone to conclude that I am a Christian. The list includes:

- A Bible verse-a-day calendar
- A polished rock with the word Pray etched in it
- Handwritten notes all over my desk with favorite Scrip-tures
- A mousepad picturing an artwork of the face of Jesus (pos-sibly sacrilegious to use as an actual mousepad, so more of a decoration)
- Three polished aluminum letters that spell D-a-d (a Father's Day gift from my favorite little urchins a few years ago)
- A wonderful collage of photos, autographed by those same kids, with Psalm 103:13 in the frame ("As a father has compassion on his children, so the Lord has compassion on those who fear him.")
- A Bible at my desk. And not one of those little New Tes-tament ones that the Gideons hand out on college cam-puses, either. This is a big honking King James Version Family Generations Heirloom Bible sitting on an antique Bible stand. (OK, just kidding; it's a little one tucked in my desk drawer. I'm a sleeper cell, after all.)

I know cubicle knickknacks are not the way to bring someone else to faith. But still, they serve a purpose. For those who are paying attention, these items are nonverbal indicators to other people of what is important to me, and maybe of the kind of person I aspire to be. I've been able to have some positive conversations with coworkers who come into my cube to talk about deeper things, I think, because of the signals I send through my actions and my office adornments.

But perhaps more importantly, these things act as a form of accountability for me. They remind me what is important while I am in this strange land. Also, if people see that this is what I aspire to, they can hold me accountable every time I say something that doesn't glorify God. Even if they don't believe in the values I do—and especially if they don't—showing everyone the faith I aspire to helps keep me accountable for my actions. Fortunately, I work in a place that allows someone to have those elements around. It's a blessing for me. And maybe for others.

Actions Speak Louder than Mousepads

I also try to stake out my faith by what I say and how I act. Unfortunately, I'm not as obvious here. Too often, I don't speak or act any differently than any of my other coworkers. I get as grouchy, gossipy, angry, and whiny as my non-Christian colleagues. I don't give others enough clues to reach the conclusion that my faith is important to me. It probably explains why I don't have more faith conversations with coworkers.

To that end, I think I would have made a miserable disciple. While Peter, James, and John were following Jesus closely, I would have been preoccupied with my needs. I could imagine the conversation:

Matthew: Hey, has anyone seen Thomas?

James: Yeah, last I saw him, he was mansplaining to the crowd why the Cubs don't have a chance this season.

Matthew: No, not Doubting Thomas. Where is Thomas the Petty and Self-Absorbed?

Andrew: Oh, he was whining that the boat seats are too hard, and the tents are drafty. Frankly, he's kind of holding us back. All in favor of not taking him to Capernaum say, "Aye."

All: Aye.

Doubting Thomas: What did I miss? Don't tell me any of you think the Cubs will make the playoffs without a pitching staff.

But I digress.

Best of Both Worlds

If I had to deduce the best way to position our work and faith, I'd say it's something along the line of bringing the best of both to the workplace. Rather than trying to compartmentalize or balance the two, going full in on both feels like the optimal approach. After all, doing excellent work at work is a way we use our God-given talents for the benefit of others, which seems like the reason we have talents in the first place. We also know that work is an opportunity to grow our faith, as we see where God has placed us, how we respond to the challenges there, and then the way we serve as the light that draws others to Christ. I don't mean to make it sound easy—it's not, as evidenced by my history of poorly executed alternatives. But I also consider it to be an interesting and fulfilling opportunity for us when we pull it off. There's something quite exhilarating about making both our Lord and our earthly boss happy.

It's all captured nicely in a verse in 1 John. He is sharing the good news in his letter that as children of God, we have both a wonderful place and a wonderful opportunity. But he also challenged his readers—and us—to not just let our faith be words but tangible examples of love. "Dear children, let us not love with words or speech but with actions and in truth" (1 John 3:18).

Acting toward others out of love seems like an appropriate way to bring our best spiritual selves and our best work selves to the same place. The truth is that I'm not doing my part. There are so many places where faith and work do align, from operating with integrity, to serving others, to sharing our lives with the people with whom we work. All it takes is a commitment to work and to faith. I pray that every year, every day, I get better at that.

In the meantime, I have ordered a lawn-sized inflatable version of Leonardo da Vinci's *Last Supper* that will surely be a conversation starter when I place it in my cube.

If that doesn't work, I can always take the Bible out of my drawer.

Section 2:
THE PEOPLE YOU MEET

Doing work generally means working with people. You can try to avoid them, but that might get in the way of doing your job. Use these simple tricks to get people to like you, do your job for you, and sign over their year-end bonuses.

CHAPTER 6:

What to Do if You Have a Boss

If you have a job, chances are good you have a boss. It is an occupational hazard of most jobs.

In my career, I've had bosses almost every time I had a job. However, during a semester in college, I completed a paid internship with a non-profit organization. During the month I was there, I never really figured out who my supervisor was. For the first few days, it was the best job ever. But it wasn't long before I started worrying, wondering what they were paying me for and what I should be doing.

It was about that time a nice man introduced himself as my boss and handed me a paycheck. I figured maybe bosses do have some value.

Before the Performance Review Was the Boss

Bosses have been around a long time, dating back to the ancient world. The word *supervisor*, for instance, comes from the ancient Aramaic. It is made up of two parts. *Super* means "big" or "grand" (or even "venti," for those of you who see the world through the lens of overpriced coffee). *Visor* means the "thing you can pull down to keep the sun out of your eyes." So *supervisor* means literally "big thing that keeps you in the dark."

That explains a lot, doesn't it?

Picking on the Boss

Even if your boss provides tremendous value to your work, sometimes we can't get past the fact that he or she is "the boss." We're conditioned not to appreciate our bosses because they represent things that we don't like: authority, structure, rules. We project onto our supervisor everything we resent about being told what to do. We react like we did when our parents told us, "You can't go to Peter's house until you clean your room," or "Stop teasing your sister," or, "No, you may not stuff green beans up your nose." That's why, to this day, my cubicle is a mess, I taunt my coworkers by repeating back, "I know you are, but what am I?", and I don't like canned vegetables, either in or out of a nasal cavity.

Bad Boss Hall of Shame

Sometimes bosses are ripe for ridicule because they deserve it. Some bosses behave so badly that they can become self-parodies. It's not clear how they became bosses, but it is clear it wasn't because of their people skills.

After extensive research, I came up with five boss types that I rate as particularly distressing. Perhaps you've experienced one of these types. (For any of my former bosses who may be reading this, let me state that I have never *personally* experienced a boss like one of these. I have just heard things from employees who aren't as fortunate as I am.)

The Micromanager: This boss seems to believe he adds the most value by focusing on useless details and painful minutiae. These bosses want to know everyone's whereabouts every minute and question every penny of expenses. It's almost as if they know they can't add value to the important stuff, so they focus on the unimportant.

A friend of mine once worked in an office where the boss was hypervigilant about working hours. When my friend, a seasoned professional in his field, tried to leave thirty minutes early for his son's soccer game, the boss followed him out to the parking lot to loudly remind him of the policy and demand that he return to work. Despite having the benefit of this kind of leadership, my friend now works elsewhere. I'm assuming the boss is still adding value to his company through his parking patrol prowess.

The Absentee Landlord: This boss is at the opposite end of the spectrum. While the Micromanager is ever-present and hovering, the Absentee boss is never to be found. She shows up once in a great while to issue some dictum or impart some awkward words of encouragement. Then she vanishes. One friend tells of having an office pool to see how long they could go without a boss sighting. I understand the record was fourteen days. Apparently, this boss assumes her greatest value is not being present. The employees are inclined to think that is probably true, when they consider what damage she might do if she did engage in the workday.

The Indecisive: This boss type can't decide what the right answer is, or sometimes what the right question is, so she lets the uncertainty hang out there, perhaps hoping the problem will solve itself. When employees want direction or guidance, they quickly realize it's a waste of time to seek input from the Indecisive boss. Sometimes the indecision is driven by a lack of confidence. Sometimes it's driven by a need to have every potential piece of data before reaching a conclusion. Whatever the cause, this boss would be better off being absentee, so at least the team can make a decision in her absence.

The Unqualified: When someone is promoted to boss, it's entirely possible that he won't have all the skills he'll need to be Super Boss. With experience, most bosses grow into the role. But the Unqualified boss just stopped growing. Or maybe moved backwards. He may bring some great attributes to the position—smiling demeanor, outgoing personality, nice hair—but professional qualifications aren't among them.

The Unqualified boss can be forgiven if he knows he needs help and reaches out to the team or his own boss for guidance and assistance. But the truly dangerous Unqualified bosses don't know that they don't know. They go blundering through work, sending teams down precisely the wrong paths. They can wreak havoc on people, department morale and the organization's operations. Employees can choose to either cover for this boss or endure the situation until he finally crashes and burns, potentially taking the organization—and their jobs—down with him. Neither option is very attractive. But before deciding to let your Unqualified boss dig his own grave, remember that the replacement potentially could be worse. You could get . . .

The Egotist: For me, the Egotist is the most distasteful kind of boss. While a well-developed self-confidence is necessary to get to the boss level, this guy takes it too far. He knows all the answers. He has seen more and done more than all the rest of the company. He finds any input from anyone else a waste of his valuable time. He thinks that God sits at *his* right hand.

Egotists wouldn't be a problem if they just kept their egos to themselves. But their wisdom, expertise, and insight demand to be shared, sometimes forcefully. And in the process, their self-centered, condescending approach can make other people feel small and miserable. They can be brusque, rude, and mean-spirited.

I always want the egotists to get their comeuppance, but they never are pulled down in a way that is quite satisfactory to me. (But then, "satisfactory" to me would probably entail some sort of public humiliation or a weekend in the stocks, which isn't really done much anymore.) In the meantime, if you ever get a chance to choose your boss, I'd scratch the Egotist from your shopping list.

Dealing with the Boss

Maybe you have an amazing, awesome boss. (In which case, why are you still reading this chapter? You can skip ahead. No one is watching to see if you read the whole book.) But if your boss isn't as awesome and amazing as mine, what do you do?

I've read up on this. Experts say you should get the perspective of others, either a mentor or one of your peers. Of course, it's often a formality, because everyone knows the boss is a jerk and you're cool. But the thought is that maybe you're just a teeny bit too close to the situation to accurately assess it. Getting an outsider's view may—just may—show that you have some role to play here. Maybe you're not communicating as you should, or not being collaborative, or not doing any of the tasks spelled out in your job description. I know, I know. At least in my career, when I had a problem supervisor (and by that, I mean, *if* I ever had a problem supervisor), I can guarantee it was 99 percent the other person. Maybe just a little, tiny bit me. But very little. I mean, hardly even measurable.

But brace yourself. If you're a Christian in the workplace, there's more. You may need to do a serious heart exam to adjust your attitude toward your boss. It may require some good old-fashioned compassion.

(Now, for my fellow members of the Pedantic Book Readers Society, let me say, yes, I know that the heart is a hollow muscle that pumps blood. But I'm going with the more poetic representation of the heart as the core of life and the center of our emotions, personality, and spirit. Don't be so literal, OK?)

Sympathy for the Boss

I only learned compassion for the boss when I became a boss. (It's amazing how sensitive you can become to other's hardships when they happen to you.) When I was an entry-level grunt, I was the last stop when work rolled downhill. It was my job to deal with obnoxious specialty advertising reps and vindictive administrative assistants. The only people who would give me the time of day were the surly cafeteria lunch ladies. And they only spoke to me to tell me to "move along."

Then, for whatever reason (longevity, most likely), one day I found myself the boss of my own little kingdom, with a single faithful subject and a budget with more money than I had thought possible to spend (though I gave it a good shot in my first year). Suddenly, I got invited to meetings. People asked for my input. Lunch ladies used my name when they told me to "move along." I had arrived!

I should have been thrilled. But instead, I discovered that being a boss meant I had to deal with icky things like hiring people and, uh, "letting someone go." I was expected to hang out with a new group of people that I frankly didn't like at all. And I had more headaches and more people demanding answers for more things that weren't even remotely within the span of my control.

The experience taught me that bosses are in a tough spot because they have more responsibility, pressure, and headaches than we mere mortals do. They are more fearful that any mistake they make will affect a lot more people, money, and market share. When you're in the mailroom and you mess up, Ms. Smith doesn't get her mail. When you're in the executive suite and you mess up, jobs are lost, share price drops, and you read about it all in column six on the front page of the *Wall Street Journal*.

Helping the Boss

Does it take a mile in someone else's shoes to have compassion for them? (That's a rhetorical question. In my case, the answer is always "yes.") As a Christian employee, my job is not to criticize or undercut the boss. It may be tempting, and I may believe I have statistically valid documentation that my boss is just the other side of useless. But that's not my role. In fact, my role is the exact opposite. I am to submit to authority, follow the boss's lead, and pray for my boss.

Obeying God

The Bible is clear that God is God, and so, by process of elimination, our earthly boss is not God. When there's a clear conflict between God and the boss, go with God. But generally, 99 percent of what our earthly bosses want is legal, moral, and nonfattening. In that case, we need to wrap our heads around the concept of placing ourselves under the authority of the person in charge. God allows people in charge to be in charge in order to carry out God's will. Our job is not to judge whether or not the right person is the boss. Our job is to respect that hierarchy.

In yet another example of how Scripture is sometimes antithetical to the work world, I consider 1 Peter 2:13–15 one of the most "in your face" pieces of Scripture on respecting authority:

> Submit yourselves for the Lord's sake to every human authority, whether to the emperor, as the supreme authority, or to governors, who are sent by him to punish those who do wrong and to commend those who do right. For it is God's will that by doing good you should silence the ignorant talk of foolish people.

Paul's letter to the Colossians gives us another example of how to deal with this. Namely, we need to keep our eyes focused on the ultimate boss. Paul characterized Jesus as head over every ruler and boss. "In Christ you have been brought to fullness. He is the head over every power and authority" (Colossians 2:10).

He drives it home in the next chapter. We shouldn't spend as much time worrying about our earthly boss as our ultimate boss. "Whatever you do, work at it with all your heart, as working for the Lord, not for human masters, since you know that you will receive an inheritance from the Lord as a reward. It is the Lord Christ you are serving" (Colossians 3:23–24).

The way I read it, we have a responsibility to serve those who hired us. While God is our ultimate boss, we bring glory to him when we serve our employers—and, by extension, our earthly bosses—with excellence.

But what do you do when your earthly boss is a knucklehead? That's a toughie. Like all difficult things, sometimes God uses knucklehead bosses to draw us closer to God. It can be an opportunity to strengthen our ability to submit our will to the plan God has for us. And because bosses are often people, sometimes God creates the situation so we are in a position to witness to them. And sometimes we're in what we believe is the wrong place at the wrong time, and we get stuck with an icky boss so we can call on God to get us out or get us through it. But in the meantime, we are called to serve responsibly while growing in obedience.

Nowhere on the list is grousing about your boss until he or she changes.

It's easy when you're in conflict with the boss to seek others' affirmation of your point of view in the me-versus-them conflict. But as Christians at work, we're called to a higher standard, a higher focus. If we truly believe in God's plan, we should believe in his ability to grow us in all circumstances, even with knuckle-head bosses.

Or so I hear.

Did I mention that all my bosses have been wonderful?

CHAPTER 7:

The Delicate Situation of Coworkers

Whether you work from home or at an office, chances are good that you have to deal with that ubiquitous feature of every workplace: coworkers. I say "ubiquitous" because describing them as "being constantly underfoot like cockroaches" sounds a bit mean (even if it is potentially accurate).

Of course, I'm kidding. Cockroaches send far fewer emails than most of my coworkers.

I'm not exactly anti-coworker. I can think of dozens of coworkers over the years with whom I have enjoyed sharing office space. The coworkers who are the easiest to love are the ones who make me feel good. They brighten my day. They make me laugh. They are friends to whom I can whine when I have a bad day. I enjoy going out to lunch with them. I'm pretty sure that's how they feel about me, although I don't get invited to lunch much anymore (not since I started referring to coworkers as "cockroaches," come to think of it).

Some of my best friends actually started out as lowly coworkers. Believe it or not.

Then there are other coworkers. They are the ones who get on my nerves. They don't pull their weight on group projects. They eat odiferous leftovers in the adjacent cube. They can't seem to figure out the video call mute button. They spend way too much time standing around colleagues' desks chitchatting (which is a sadly underused term, and using it in no way indicates that I am a fuddy-duddy).

Because I am not really a "people-person" (big surprise, right?), I tend to see coworkers as an obstacle to getting work done. They add complexity to work, slowing things down and introducing uncertainty into project outcomes. They interrupt, question conclusions, and offer suggestions for how things can be done differently, even though my process works just fine. If it weren't for the coworkers I enjoy, I'd be perfectly happy to only see coworkers in the company directory.

Building a Coworker Wall

Given my perspective, it's probably not surprising that I am very intentional about keeping my distance from coworkers. Online or in person, I show up late to meetings to avoid having to make small talk. When I am working at my desk in the office, I send subtle signals that I do not want to interact with others. I usually wear headphones, for instance, so coworkers assume I am on a call. I also wear sunglasses, a scarf, and one of those big wool

Eskimo hats with the flaps pulled down to make them think twice about showing me pictures of their new puppy.

When I work from home, I also send small signals that I do not want to interact. If someone instant-messages me, I generally wait at least a day before responding, which significantly reduces the "instant-ness" of the message. On video calls, I leave my camera off and stay on mute. But I also leave a gas-powered leaf blower running near my desk, so when someone asks me to come off mute to add my input, the sound is so loud that everyone quickly asks me to re-mute. It's an effective technique. Over time, I've gotten accustomed to the pounding headaches and blurred vision. It's a small price to pay for keeping my distance.

Taking a Different Approach

Unfortunately, I have recognized recently that my methodology for navigating coworker interactions is potentially flawed. I had a stunning indication of that when I learned of a coworker's battle with cancer. I had noticed that she had been absent from project meetings for several weeks, but I ascribed her absence to being busy, or failing to manage her time, or excessive chitchatting. I had to do some significant soul-searching when I realized she was making a valiant (and eventually successful) fight for her life right under my nose. But my desire to not engage meant I missed that opportunity to serve and be supportive.

Not surprisingly, reading any amount of Scripture further indicates that my coworkers-at-arm's-length approach is lacking. Even a cursory reading of the Bible reveals that people are the reason we are on Earth. Other people are not something that gets in the way of our true purpose; *they are our purpose.*

Paul tells the Ephesians, for instance, that they are to live a life worthy of their calling, which includes heartfelt connection with others. "Be completely humble and gentle; be patient, bearing with one another in love. Make every effort to keep the unity of the Spirit through the bond of peace" (Ephesians 4:2–3). Paul concludes the chapter with a call for the same grace that Jesus shows us: "Get rid of all bitterness, rage and anger, brawling and slander, along with every form of malice. Be kind and compassionate to one another, forgiving each other, just as in Christ God forgave you" (Ephesians 4:31–32).

He challenged the Galatians in the same way when he repeats Jesus's command to love our neighbors: "You, my brothers and sisters, were called to be free. But do not use your freedom to indulge the flesh; rather, serve one another humbly in love. For the entire law is fulfilled in keeping this one command: 'Love your neighbor as yourself'" (Galatians 5:13-15).

He says something similar about connectedness in his letter to the Romans: "Rejoice with those who rejoice; mourn with those who mourn. Live in harmony with one another . . ." (Romans 12:15–16).

There's a whole lot of "one another" in those Scriptures. I don't get to hunker down and avoid others yet claim that I am living in God's will. I fought it as long as I could. But I eventually realized I needed to change my attitude about my coworkers.

Shifting to an Outward Focus

I'm taking small steps to reorient my view. But even if they are small, they are steps nonetheless. It started with a decision to do something different. I decided that I need to be intentional about serving my colleagues. I need to set aside the ease of ignoring what is going on around me and engage with others. And I need to keep at it, giving myself grace on the days when I just really, really am not feeling it.

I also need to listen. People are pretty much open books, but we must stop what we're doing to hear what they are saying. Sometimes the true hearing comes between the words of what people verbalize, or even in what they don't say. The only way to pick up on that is to practice serious listening. In my case, that means I use the gaps between when I speak to actually listen to what the other person is saying, and not just use the time to plan what I will say when it's my turn to talk again.

Practicing intentional listening, I learned recently that a coworker's daughter was struggling in college and was at risk of dropping out. The situation was causing stress for my colleague, who wanted what was best for his daughter but also struggled with what impact the situation would have on his daughter's career prospects and self-esteem. The coworker initially didn't volunteer the information, but I saw signs of the stress in his life, which prompted me to stop to truly listen and note the shift in his demeanor. I would have missed the opportunity to come alongside to encourage him if I had followed my traditional hands-off approach.

Another habit I am trying to adopt is the ability to be vulnerable. Now, this is a tough one. I was born in a family that didn't just frown on crying (ironic, right?) but actively mocked it. As a child, I remember tearfully telling a family gathering about a teenage bully who had thrown snowballs at my friends and me as we walked home from school. My younger brother, who must have been about six at the time, proudly told the table of relatives that if that had happened to him, he would have turned around and "beaten them silly!" The family guffawed and held him up as the hero, telling me I should be more like my baby brother. Lesson learned: Bravado is more prized than vulnerability. (The rest of the story is that when he turned seven, my brother did "beat silly" the town bully, apparently indicating the bully wasn't as big a threat as

I had perceived. But Mom grounded my brother for crossing the street to do it, so I found some satisfaction in that.)

Fortunately, as an adult, I have learned that being vulnerable actually gets easier. As we get older, we have less to prove to others and more easily recognize that everyone is struggling with something (or, in my case, many somethings). I have realized it's really hard to get through life without experiencing some kind of trauma that shapes you or scares you or throws you off the path that you were planning to follow. And while there is security in knowing of God's care and promises when that happens, the power of caring colleagues can be particularly precious in the moment. The people we see every day can respond and react in a very intimate way if we are willing to allow that to happen.

As he challenged the Romans, Paul extended a simple, similar challenge to the Galatians. "Carry each other's burdens, and in this way you will fulfill the law of Christ" (Galatians 6:2). It's hard to carry one another's burdens if you don't know what they are.

Thinking of a Word That Begins with "L"

Finally, you should tell people you love them.

I mean, I would never do that, but you totally should. For someone like me, who works to keep people at arm-and-leg-and-torso's-length, professing to love others is a mile too far. But I have taken small steps here, too. I have gotten to the point where I can now say, "I hope you're doing well." Or on occasion, I have said, "I think you're heading in the right direction." In a moment of exuberance, undoubtedly caused by a righteous filling of the Holy Spirit, I once told a colleague, "I appreciate you." I had to go lie down afterward. But I am sure my colleague was moved and inspired by my outpouring of affection. (Assuming he recognized that I was being sincere and not my usual sarcastic self. If he's reading this now, let me assure him I was being sincere.)

Words matter, and affirmative words matter a great deal.

Motivation for U-Turns

If you're like me, orchestrating this dramatic change of heart is a tall hill to climb. I have made a profession of ignoring my coworkers, avoiding them, and pretending to be unpleasant so they don't stop to talk. (Yes, *pretending*.) Why would I change to engage with them?

First, it's the right thing to do (see the Scripture above).

Second (and here, finally, I can get back to making it about me), I feel good when I do it. I may be inclined to ignore or distance myself from my coworkers, but that takes an incredible amount of energy. If you're a human being, you are wired to be social, to be connected to others. Even an introvert like me—whose batteries drain the more time I spend in groups—can savor relationships with individuals I trust and for whom I care, sometimes deeply. The only way I find those few precious folks is by opening up when I come into contact with new faces.

The workplace is a natural landscape in which to do this. Our coworkers are people we see frequently and work alongside to accomplish tasks, so eventually it gets harder to pretend we have no reason to share. From the sheer volume of time we spend with these people, we get to know them, whether we like it or not. Why not go all the way to truly invest in one another?

The work environment also runs much more smoothly when we engage with our coworkers. I may claim to be more effective when I work alone, but that's malarkey. No matter how many skills I may think I have, I can never have all the skills—let alone all the time, all the experiences, and all the education—that the team has. Done right, the workplace can become the kind of place that Paul described to the Romans, the Corinthians, and the Ephesians, where the diversity of gifts come together to make a complete and effective corporate body. My failure to engage, contribute my gifts, and help nurture the gifts of others is kind of the opposite of community. When I do engage, the work goes more smoothly, everyone is more productive, and it's just easier to get work done. I sometimes have to remind myself of this, so I don't pull the disappearing trick. I also know in my heart it's the truth.

This whole exploration has caused me to change my perspective on coworkers. The vast majority of them still frustrate, annoy, and exasperate me. I'm learning to see their giftedness when I see them through God's lens. They are blessed children of God, each seeking to use their giftedness for something greater than themselves.

But would it kill you to stop all the chitchatting?

CHAPTER 8

Adoring the "Hard to Adores"

I n every job, in every family, in every community, there are people who are just not easy to like. In some cases, it isn't even easy to be in the same room with them. Or on a conference call. They rub you the wrong way, kind of like a porcupine rubs you the wrong way when you drag it across your tongue. (There are some things you just need to trust me on.)

I'm guessing you can think of at least one of these special people at work. It might be the coworker who complains constantly about her compensation, about other colleagues, or about you. Sometimes while you're standing right there. It might be the executive who calls to demand answers at any time of the day or night, regardless of what holiday it is. It might be the customer who is never happy with the products you sell, the hours you're open, or the size of your parking lot. And this unhappy customer returns again and again, just so you know the depth of his unhappiness!

These unpleasant types have been around as long as there have been people. The Bible is chock-full of examples (Exhibit A: Cain). Jesus met many difficult characters who were major spoilsports. (The Pharisees, the Romans, and the demon-possessed guys in the tombs come to mind). Esther and Mordecai surely wished they had never met Haman. David was beyond patient with King Saul, given the spears Saul lobbed in David's general direction. And special recognition goes to Moses, who put up with a whole nation of grumblers and whiners following him around the desert. His forty years of patience may take the longevity record for dealing with the unpleasant class.

Labeling the Species

Given the pervasiveness of these characters, I was drawn to an endearing term I heard to describe these contentious souls. One might call these disagreeable people the "Hard-to-Adores."

I like that phrase because it doesn't assume that *no one* could appreciate these loathsome individuals. They are not called the "Inconceivable-to-Adores," after all. Calling them "Hard-to-Adores" also sets the expectation that we should at least *try* to adore them. The only way we know they are hard to adore is if we first give it some effort. But the phrase also gives me an out if I don't adore them. I tried, but, well, it just didn't happen. That's certainly understandable. After all, they are "hard to adore."

Making a List

I seem to attract a lot of "Hard-to-Adores." (Or perhaps I just have a special gift for recognizing them.) They come in a variety of formats. Sometimes they are "Hard-to-Adore" because of their grating behaviors, such as arguing, yelling, or yelling while arguing. Sometimes "Hard-to-Adores" earn the title because they see the workplace as a battlefield or a boxing ring, a place to create and foster conflict. I don't want to say they are demonic, but you can't help but notice a similar playbook.

Sometimes these individuals are motivated by something a little more worldly, like doing whatever it takes to advance their careers, regardless of the impact on other people. They can be singularly focused and overly aggressive to the point that you don't want to be on the same org chart with them, let alone the same cubicle.

Some people are on a universal "Hard-to-Adore" list. People who are mean-spirited, ruthless, steal from Salvation Army kettles, and never use a turn signal are almost always "Hard-to-Adores." And if they press it, they could easily step up to an elevated "Impossible-to-Adore" category.

The amount of interaction you have with the public, the type of work you do, and the phase of the moon may determine how many "Hard-to-Adores" you encounter on a given day. I was a bit taken aback to realize that, for me, almost everyone fits into the "Hard-to-Adore" category at some point. Maybe I have unreasonably high standards. (I happen to think perfection is achievable for most people if they would only put their backs into it.) Even my loving wife and charming children fit into this category on some days. But the fact that they tend to attain that status on days when I have placed most of the North American population in that category might, maybe, possibly say more about me than about them.

Responding to the "Hard-to-Adores"

Let's assume I'm not the only one who sees "Hard-to-Adores" around the conference room. If you also experience this class of coworkers, you need to have a plan for how you will respond. I have taken several approaches. The safest is to avoid them. Hide when you see them in the office. Wear earbuds and always pretend to be on a call when they are around. Simulate technical difficulties when they are on a video call with you.

Yes, I know this approach flies in the face of my realization in the last chapter about the value of coworkers. But the rules feel different for the "Hard-to-Adores." Taking this approach is actually beneficial for these characters. Lack of contact tends to soften my perception of their rough edges and prevents me from doing anything that will irreparably harm our relationship.

Unfortunately, sometimes distancing myself is neither possible nor desirable, especially if the "Hard-to-Adore" in question signs my paycheck.

The opposite approach is to confront them. Point out in clear, direct terms that they are horrible, obnoxious people. Be sure to provide sufficient detail on their shortcomings so there will be no misunderstanding of their faults. Then stand back and receive their flowing appreciation for all you have done to help them be better people. (I'm kidding. This is a terrible idea. Someone can get seriously hurt that way.)

Even if I am not actively running away, I often take a passive approach with "Hard-to-Adores." That can take several forms. I can quietly undermine them by frequently asking everyone we work with if they think the person is "hard to adore." I also sigh dramatically during meetings when they talk. Or I may sit and fume, wishing God would give them a taste of their own medicine. I want an Old Testament response. I want God to give me the same satisfaction he gave Daniel as he watched King Darius toss the counselors into the lion's den after they manipulated things to get Daniel thrown in there. Or I imagine asking for what I call the

"Jeremiah Option," repeating the prophet's pleas for God to deal with the "Hard-to-Adores" who refused to believe his prophecies.

> So give their children over to famine; hand them over to the power of the sword. Let their wives be made childless and widows; let their men be put to death, their young men slain by the sword in battle. Let a cry be heard from their houses when you suddenly bring invaders against them, for they have dug a pit to capture me and have hidden snares for my feet. *(Jeremiah 18:21–22)*

I'm thinking Jeremiah was struggling with a little PPS: Post-Prophecy Stress.

Choosing a Better Path

While it might be tempting to take an Old Testament approach to the "Hard-to-Adores" in our lives, I believe God wants us to take a New Covenant approach, drawing much more on love, grace, and mercy.

Paul (himself quite the "Hard-to-Adore" while he was in that Saul-persecuting-Christians-to-death phase) gives us a model for responding to the "Hard-to-Adores." "If your enemy is hungry, feed him; if he is thirsty, give him something to drink. In doing this, you will heap burning coals on his head. Do not be overcome by evil, but overcome evil with good" (Romans 12:20–21, NASB). It's an interesting approach, essentially killing with kindness.

He also counsels us to take ourselves out of our own emotions and act in a way fitting a disciple of Jesus. "A servant of the Lord must not quarrel but must be kind to everyone, be able to teach, and be patient with difficult people" (2 Timothy 2:24, NLT).

Jesus outlined a purely kind response in the Sermon on the Mount. "But I tell you, love your enemies and pray for those who persecute you, that you may be children of your Father in heaven" (Matthew 5:44–45).

Luke's version says the same thing, with action verbs like love, bless, and pray. "But to you who are listening I say: Love your enemies, do good to those who hate you, bless those who curse you, pray for those who mistreat you" (Luke 6:27–28).

According to these verses, there seems to be a corresponding relationship between how hard a person is to adore and the effort I should make to adore him or her. The harder they are to adore, the more I need to shift my thinking. It's hard, but it's also powerful. I will never change my perspective through force of will. I need to submit and be obedient to what is pretty clear teaching. That submission starts with my mindset.

If embracing your "Hard-to-Adore" seems too daunting, I suggest starting small. To begin, see the "Hard-to-Adore" as a real, live person (assuming they are, of course). This person undoubtedly has loves, joys, sorrows, and hurts. Our task is to get close enough to recognize this fact.

Some of my favorite transformations from "Hard-to-Adore" to "Able-to-Adore" happened when I simply spent time with that person. It may not be easy to do at first, but it can be very effective in defusing the tension. An article I read by a psychologist said the key to building a relationship with someone with whom you differ is to find common ground. You do that when you spend time together and share common experiences. You develop a relationship with someone when you see them react to an experience the same way you do. Once I realize we share a common concern or can even laugh together, my attitude changes. I can see that perhaps this "Hard-to-Adore" really is a child of God, like me. I still may be challenged by this person's idiosyncrasies or frustrating habits. But I start seeing him or her in a new light, appreciating his or her strengths and understanding his or her hurts.

Even though Jesus knew some people would never accept his message, he certainly found plenty of time for many "Hard-to-Adores." I may need to turn over to him those people who frustrate me so much that, left on my own, I will avoid, or undercut, or intentionally break the relationship.

Above all else, I must consciously choose to back away from my natural snarky, selfish response to someone different than me. I have to remind myself to be compassionate, gracious, and patient. I need to recognize that, in some cases, the sandal might just be on the other foot, so to speak. As hard as it might be to imagine, I might be a "Hard-to-Adore" to that other person. They might not see me as the wonderful, gracious, generous person I am.

Because, you know, some people are just so judgmental.

CHAPTER 9

Making Others Feel Valued

There is a man who works in my office who always lifts my spirits and brightens my day. Oddly enough, whenever he sees me, he comments about my height.

"I think you're getting shorter," he'll say, or, "Didn't you used to be taller? I think you're shrinking. Maybe I'm getting taller." This always makes me laugh because I'm over six feet tall, and Benny, I believe, aspires to be five feet tall.

Whenever we work together on a project, Benny always has some funny remark that prevents me from taking myself too seriously. He immigrated to the United States from Southeast Asia, and he enjoys poking fun at Americans for our laziness, sense of self-importance, and spendthrift ways.

"You Americans think you're so great," he'll say in mock indignation. "But you pay extra for shredded lettuce and hard-boiled eggs!" Then he'll cackle that laugh of his, and I can't help but laugh along.

Benny also has a heart as big as all outdoors. He is always willing to work harder and longer than anyone else, even if the project isn't his. He stops at my desk periodically to see if there are any projects he can help with. He always has time to talk and joke with other people.

Benny is a one-of-a-kind, kindhearted, generous soul who cares more for others than he cares for himself. When Jesus told us in Matthew 5 that we need to be the light of the world, shining so that others would see the deeds of our Father (see Matthew 5:16), I think he was talking about the kinds of things Benny does. Benny isn't just a light; he's a beacon.

I hate him for that.

Well, that's probably a bit strong. I don't hate him; I just sometimes want to "smush" a break-room donut in his face. I'm not proud of that, of course. I have that disconcerting reaction because he is doing the good that I want to do, but I just never seem to find a way to do it. What I need to actually "smush" is my own sinful, selfish nature that prevents me from being more like Benny. I want to take it out on Benny because he represents what I'm not. (It's that kind of maturity that makes me think I'm destined to be a senior executive.)

Benny is doing what Jesus told us to do when he said, "Love your neighbor as yourself" (Matthew 22:39) and "Greater love has no one than this, that he lay down his life for his friends" (John 15:13). Or, as Paul said in 1 Timothy 4:16, "Watch your life and doctrine closely. Persevere in them, because if you do, you will save both yourself and your hearers."

And in my frequent downhill slaloms from towering conceit to self-recrimination, I realize I'm not living out Jesus's commands to be that light on the lampstand.

Judging Others Harshly

I'm chronically hampered in letting my light shine for others because I compete with other people. I compare my own attributes to theirs and judge them severely, so I look better. (A colleague once said, "If you want to look good, stand next to someone ugly." Judging other people harshly is my way of making them ugly and myself more attractive. As I said before, I've got "senior executive" written all over me.)

Rather than take responsibility for that kind of behavior, I can make any number of excuses about why I do this: poor parenting, mean teachers, fluoride in the water. But that doesn't matter. What matters is that my behavior falls far short of the standard set by Jesus . . . or even Benny.

Just Wanting to be Seen

Making others feel valued is really important because it gets to our role as Christians in the workplace. We have a unique and special opportunity to share the Good News with coworkers. And in this topsy-turvy world of work, with the quiet quitting, social inequity, and seeking meaning through work, coworkers want to know that they matter. They—and we—want to be seen and affirmed.

I read a writer once who said that of course people matter to God. But before people can accept God's love, they first need to see that they matter to other people. That's a role we play.

If you've paid attention at all, you know we should be evangelizing others with the amazing story of God's love we have to share. But if you're like me, when you hear "evangelizing," you think of a big tent revival in the conference room with a line of baptisms to follow at the watercooler. Anything less than that feels somehow lacking. While that kind of direct outreach is certainly needed—and I've seen coworkers who can share the glory of Jesus Christ with compassion and grace without taking their eyes off their laptops—I don't think we should ever underestimate the power of simply acknowledging others, serving others, and seeing others. Those things have value even if the interaction doesn't end with a baptism before the weekly staff meeting.

I get excited about this approach because, even with my messy, sinful nature, I can do that. I can't seem to do it consistently, and I don't have the social graces to carry on small talk for more than, say, eighteen seconds. But I can smile. I can say, "Good morning." I can ask how someone's day is going, and then stop what I'm doing long enough to hear the answer. And I believe that matters and shouldn't be discounted in our ministry.

Turning Up the Illumination

But how do I do that more often?

Well, for starters, I don't believe *I* can. If it's left up to me, I'll just keep on being a jerk. It goes back to that selfish, sinful nature that makes me do what I don't really want to do but keep doing anyway, while the good I want to do I can't seem to get around to, uh, really doing. The only way I can hope to change that is by surrendering my will, confessing to and seeking forgiveness for those I have wronged, and giving the steering wheel back to God. It takes a good self-talking-to at times, reminding myself that I am called—and equipped—to serve others as a believer in Christ.

For my analytical mind, I need a plan. I think there are three things I can reasonably do that could make a big difference to others. The first is seeing other people.

This suggestion may seem silly because, unless you have a visual impairment or are blindfolded as part of your job, of course you see people. But do you? I am flabbergasted (yet another word that doesn't get used enough; I'm doing my part) that at the end of the day, I can have a hard time remembering with whom I worked that day. I am usually so focused on my work and my needs that I sorta kinda miss noticing the people around me.

That phenomenon reveals itself when I meet someone for the first time and they go on and on about how much they enjoyed working with me on that team two years ago, when we reorganized the payroll functions, and even though it was hard, it was a great experience, and we got a great result, and didn't I think so, too? As they're talking, *I'm thinking, I did work on that project . . . but did she? I don't remember her.* So I assume she's staging some elaborate ruse or *Candid Camera* episode rather than recognizing that the problem lies in my failure to truly see others.

Second, once you stop to notice the people with whom you interact, you need to know their needs. There are two ways to gather this information. You can hand them a form, identifying their needs by category, and ask them to fill it out. A slightly less awkward method is to listen when they speak. While the first method is certainly easier for you and likely more complete, apparently it smacks of "glaring insincerity and cluelessness" (or so I was told). The better option is to listen. Really listen.

I was having a conversation with a colleague recently when she shared that it was a tough week. Her husband's grandfather, a beloved member of their hometown community, had died. She and her husband would make the drive home at the end of the workweek to be with family and attend services. I expressed sympathy and compassion (because everyone knows that's what you're supposed to do). But by the end of the conversation a few minutes later, looking to wrap things up, I asked in a singsong voice, "So, any big plans for the weekend?" She sat stoned-faced and said, "Well, aside from going to the funeral, no." I was mortified. It was yet another example of the way I can sometimes participate in work conversations without really hearing what is being said.

The third step is to take action to make it real. That can mean several things. It can mean praying for the people I work with about their needs. It can also mean writing down the personal thoughts people share so I don't rely on my ego-centered memory to remember to ask about their concerns when we meet next. I've found that sometimes acting first is a good way to bring my thinking along, too.

Two of my favorite illustrations of making people feel valued come from the book of Acts. The first takes place in Acts 8. Philip is in Samaria (home of those dreaded Samaritans). He was having a great ministry there, preaching the Good News, casting out demons, making a foundation for a strong church. But God sent him in a new direction to meet one person who needed to know God. He meets the Ethiopian eunuch and explains to him the contents of Isaiah, eventually baptizing him along the road. This story speaks to me about the power that comes with ministering to one person, refuting my mistaken belief that I am only doing good if I am serving rooms full of people.

The second example hits a little closer to home. In Acts 10, Peter is working hard not to minister to Gentiles, citing the precedent in the law. He has a bias for the Jewish people, probably because he is one. But God gives Peter a vision of eating all kinds of foods, including those that the law had previously labeled impure or unclean. God was showing Peter that he didn't get to choose to whom he ministered, that the Good News applies to all. I connect with that illustration because I tend to be pretty choosy about who gets my attention or TLC. I usually focus on people most like me. Apparently ministering exclusively to people exactly like me and ignoring people not like me is not God's will. Like Peter, sometimes I only realize it when God makes it so clear that even I can't miss it.

Covered in Grace

Most of all, I take great solace in the fact that Christ offered me his grace, so I have hope that every time I fall, I can try again.

Because here's the sobering part: I don't know if Benny is a Christian. I know he's a nice guy who cares for others, but I don't know what motivates his kindness. So if my coworkers compare Benny, who never has a coarse word for anyone, and me, the proclaimed follower of Jesus, incapable of speaking of others without using words like *jerk*, then my witness isn't going to measure up.

This is doubly important because we represent God in the workplace. Jesus's full commandment in Matthew 5:16 is to "let your light shine before men in such a way that they may see your good works and glorify your Father who is in heaven" (NASB). We are meant to be lights to other people so that they are drawn to the Creator of light. Only through grace could I hope to be such a powerful draw to others.

In the meantime, I work hard to learn from the example of Benny, with his generous, overflowing care and concern for others. And while I can behave more like Benny (and Jesus), I shouldn't forget that I am already contributing to our relationship.

For instance, I can reach things for him on the top shelf.

Section 3:
Avoiding the Daily Pitfalls

Given the different perspectives of work and faith, it's quite possible you'll get tripped up when you try to live your faith at work. Identifying the pitfalls is the first step. Not stepping in the pits is the second, uh, step on the path to not pitfalling.

CHAPTER 10:

Leadership Is Harder
without Followers

T he first time my employer bestowed staff leadership responsibilities on me, I was ecstatic. After years of toiling at the bottom rungs of the organization as an individual contributor, I was finally recognized for my superior ability and strategic intellect. With a single payroll change authorization, I would now have unlimited power. No longer would I have to take direction from people who didn't know what they were doing. Now I would be able to make the rules, assign the projects, drive the initiatives. I finally would be able to assemble resources to achieve my master plan of customer accumulation and competitor domination. More importantly, I would now have access to immeasurable wealth and elevated status worthy of my incredible giftedness.

In hindsight, my reaction might have been a tad over the top.

After all, I was being promoted to senior communications specialist with a single direct report. There would be no unlimited power or immeasurable wealth. In fact, given that the new responsibility consisted mostly of reminding my direct report every two weeks to turn in her time sheet or she wouldn't get paid, arguably it was a step backward.

Misunderstanding Leadership

From underneath, leadership look can look pretty awesome, with greater responsibility, a team of people to guide, and accountability for much more than your own activities. But from the leadership seat, leadership can be daunting, with greater responsibility, a team of people to guide, and accountability for much more than your own activities. I desperately wanted to be a leader when I wasn't one. When I was one, I discovered that leadership entailed a lot more than I anticipated. And not in a good way.

I had assumed that leadership was all about the perks: the position, the pay, the power. When I became a leader, I realized that it entailed a list of tasks and a sense of responsibility that was far beyond what I had conceived. And far beyond what I wanted. Suddenly, people were looking to me for answers! They asked me for direction! They were depending on me for the resources to do what needed to be done. I began asking others for advice on how to navigate this new role.

I need to acknowledge that leaders aren't only people who supervise other people. You can be a leader in whatever role you have in an organization, from leading project groups to being a model of the company culture. In those cases, you can also slip out of the leadership role if you decide you just want to ride in the passenger seat for a while. But when you supervise people, that's when you are truly tied to the leader role. It's a lot harder to pretend you're no longer a leader when you're responsible for approving someone's time sheet. (Ask the people who went without a paycheck the week I forgot to approve time sheets before I left for vacation.)

Leader as Steward

The best piece of advice I got when I was appointed to lead people is that leadership is not about the leader; it's about the followers. It's a simple concept, and probably self-evident to people who are more self-aware than I am. That counsel really stuck with me because it's so counter to what I believed about leadership before I got there.

In one of his *Life for Leaders* devotions for the De Pree Center, Mark Roberts talks about leadership as caring. He quotes a colleague describing leadership as serving "the people entrusted to your care."[3] The organization may characterize them as "full-time equivalents" or "resources," but they are real, live people who need and deserve attention and care.

Leadership is more than exercising authority. It includes guiding, listening, and demonstrating empathy. It means putting others' needs ahead of your own. Some might even call it "love," but that's an emotional depth I can't quite bring myself to express in public, being raised in the Upper Midwest and all.

They don't teach you that perspective in leadership seminars. (Although, who knows, maybe they do. I went straight to the sessions on "Selecting the Right Luxury Vehicle for Your Leadership Style.") An effective leader needs to find the balance between accomplishing the organizational objectives and nurturing the team he or she leads. And if it's done right, leadership can be a pretty fantastic thing. I've experienced leaders who lead with grace, care, and compassion. These are people who lead with humility, who see leadership as an honor and a privilege. They are truly other-focused and, as one of their followers, it made me want to go where they led.

Unfortunately, that's not something that comes naturally to one as self-absorbed as I am.

Having a Stable Foundation

Aside from putting others' interests ahead of my own, I also struggled as a leader when I heard criticism from the team.

One of my leadership low points came when I received an email from the husband of one of the team members I was supposed to be leading. He didn't intend to email me. He was responding to his wife, who had forwarded to him a team email I had sent out. She sent it to him with a snarky comment, and he replied to me, thinking he was replying to her, with an equally snarky response about my, uh, leadership abilities. It might have been a more humiliating experience for me than it was for him (although I understand the snarky couple had quite the conversation over dinner that evening).

"Feedback" from the team is just one of the challenges leaders face. There's the need to make tough decisions (and the need not to overreact when those decisions are second-guessed), share bad news, motivate exhausted team members, provide guidance without micromanaging, fix problems without demoralizing everyone, and try to steer the group in a direction no one wants to go. There were days in my leadership role when I felt the problems were running at me like the bulls in Pamplona. And, silly me, those were the days I decided it would be a good idea to tie my shoelaces together.

Which led to the second-best piece of advice I received: Leadership is only for the spiritually strong.

Prayed-Up Leadership

Being an effective leader means consistently bringing your best every day. That means finding a balance between being too caught up in the ego-feeding perks on the one hand and being discouraged by the challenges and grumblings on the other. To do that, I believe a leader has to be grounded in his or her core values if he or she is going to demonstrate grace and kindness when there are so many things happening to discourage both. Being grounded means getting out of your own way, rising above pride and insecurities to be focused on others. It's not easy. I was frantically scribbling notes one Sunday morning when our pastor gave a great prescription for how to achieve that: Being grounded requires abiding in Jesus.

Abide is a challenging word. Our pastor described it as lining up with the heart of God, so that we see the world the way God sees it. Abiding is being plugged into God, starting, living and ending each day in the presence of Jesus. It's a challenge, because, well, the world has other ideas about where you should reside. I, for one, relish my time in Pride Land, at the center of Self-Centered Town. I have an over-the-top vacation property in All-About-Me, USA. Hanging out in those places pushes God to the periphery and makes my leadership unstable, tottering between pride and being overwhelmed by the problems I see.

I'm grateful our pastor didn't stop there by challenging us to "abide," because it's hard to know what that looks and feels like. Fortunately, he shared the kinds of things that can help us get there. And they are practical things we can do: reading the Bible, reading and watching Christian authors and speakers, praying, meditating, and worshipping. Of course, it's not always easy to maintain a steady diet of spiritual disciplines. We have to keep at it and celebrate the progress when it occurs. But I have to remind myself that it's much easier for me to accomplish those practical actions than just try to be holy all the time.

Jesus as Leader Extraordinaire

It also helps that we have an example of what effective leadership really looks like. The greatest example of leader—probably ever—is Jesus. He is the literal definition of a servant leader. Even just a reading of the Gospel subheads reveals how he effectively led a band of misfits to accomplish an unbelievable task: introducing the world to God. (If you really want a detailed listing of the leadership traits Jesus exemplified, I recommend *Leadership Lessons of Jesus* by Bob Briner and Ray Pritchard. They provide dozens of examples of the right things Jesus did as a leader that will be very helpful to follow if you are in any kind of leadership role.)

One of the great leadership stories that Jesus shared was the story of the Good Samaritan. You probably can recite the story. Jesus's Gospel parable is a staple of Sunday school classes and Bible studies. But the parable about serving also offers lessons for leaders.

> But a Samaritan, as he traveled, came where the man was; and when he saw him, he took pity on him. He went to him and bandaged his wounds, pouring on oil and wine. Then he put the man on his own donkey, took him to an inn and took care of him. The next day he took out two silver coins and gave them to the innkeeper. "Look after him," he said, "and when I return, I will reimburse you for any extra expense you may have." *(Luke 10:33–35)*

I find three themes in the story that can apply to leadership:
1. **Be bold**. The Samaritan doesn't do his work anonymously. He doesn't drop the traveler at the doorstep, ring the

doorbell, and run away. Jesus tells us that the Samaritan asks the innkeeper to look after the injured traveler. The Samaritan takes accountability for the traveler's care. His example provides a model to consider how we could visibly demonstrate care for the fellow travelers that we lead.

2. **Be generous.** This aspect of the story has always bothered me (which reveals a level of personal frugality that would make my parsimonious ancestors proud). The Samaritan not only gives the innkeeper two silver coins but declares that he will provide more if it's needed. The question is raised: "What do the people I lead want from me?" It might be compensation (which I haven't seen anyone turn down yet). More often, it is my time—an often rarer and more valued commodity. Am I able to say to people I lead, "Here are two hours of my time, and if that's not enough, I'll be back tomorrow with more"?

3. **Be committed.** After convicting me of my own lack of generosity, this story also unmasks my tendency to only meet the minimum requirement of commitment. In contrast, the Samaritan does much more. He spends the night tending to the injured man, and then arranges to come back to check on him when he returns from further travels. The Samaritan makes a serious commitment. I have to ask myself, "How does the team I lead know that I'm committed to them for the long haul? How can I show that I will not abandon them, saving myself (my ego, my reputation, my career) when the going gets tough?"

If you're in a leadership role, the people you lead may not be lying on the roadside stripped of their clothes and injured (and if they are, then it's probably only a matter of time before you will get a call from HR). But they would probably appreciate a leader who lives out the elements Jesus taught in the Samaritan story. Otherwise, they may find other leaders to follow.

Which brings me to the third piece of advice I got when I was a leader: "If you think you're leading, but no one is following you, then you are only taking a walk."

Apparently, my dreams of unlimited power and immeasurable wealth will have to wait.

CHAPTER 11:

The Hazard of Comparing Ourselves to Others

One of the more charming elements of the modern work-place is the conducive environment it provides for com-paring yourself to others. Sometimes it feels like we are all in one big cage match, competing with one another for jobs, status, resources, and promotions. As a result, we feel compelled to continually check out one another's progress. We need to know how much of the boss's attention we're getting or how fast our career is advancing compared to our peers. There's a built-in incen-tive to continually check the rearview mirror—or heaven forbid, look ahead—to see where everyone else is.

As if I need any more incentive to do that.

I'm constantly comparing myself to others. Who's up? Who's down? Who got to add headcount in their department? Who sat at the same table as the regional director at the company picnic? Who wiped out with a gaffe-filled presentation to the board of directors? Every little thing is a potential metric by which I can compare myself to others. And the worse the metric makes them look compared to me, well, giddy up.

Accumulation Anticipation

My tendency to contrast my situation with others' is in full force on the topic of "stuff." I am always keenly aware of what other people have relative to me. I have been officially diagnosed with an ailment called ECE: Excessively Covetous Eyesight. I want what I don't have. If someone else has it, I want it twice as much. Unfortunately, at last count, I believe I'm one of about eight billion people worldwide afflicted with this ailment.

It's particularly telling that I usually don't want something until I see that someone else has it. I didn't realize I needed an array of computer monitors on my desk until I saw a coworker with more screens than Best Buy. I never knew I needed a flashy luxury sports car until another friend got one. It was so quiet! So clean! The windows rolled down without a crank! I tried to convince my wife that my ancient car was long overdue for replacement. She countered with similar concerns that her husband, much older than his car, was also looking rough around the edges and probably should be traded up.

I backed off. She plays dirty.

Comparing Careers

My tendency to compare myself to others is in full bloom at work. Given how incredibly important my career is to me (yes, I know what an idol is—this is nothing like that, and I'm embarrassed for you that you brought it up), it's not surprising to me that I spend so much time contrasting my progress relative to others. There are so many scales by which I measure my standing. I check out my title, my position, the prominence of my department in the year-end accomplishments report. I don't have access to other people's salaries (the data revealed in the painful Salary Memo Incident of 2014 has gotten quite dated), so I have to look for clues, such as the cars they drive, the clothes they wear, or the vacations they take. Of course, the major area in which I compare myself to others is how fast and how far my career is moving ahead compared to theirs. How long were they in their job before they got promoted? How many salary levels is my position ahead of theirs? What's their title? Their supervisor's title?

Let me be clear: I am not proud of this. It's gritty, unseemly, and gauche. The fact that I know this and do it anyway probably doesn't make me look very good in your eyes. Unfortunately, if that's the case, I think you have pretty good eyesight.

A Better Biblical Model

Not surprisingly, Jesus had some words about our tendency to compare ourselves to others. One of the most frustrating (to me, at least) is in the illustration he shared in Matthew 20. It's often called the parable of the workers in the vineyard, but I've always preferred to call it "the parable of the crazy farmer."

Jesus says the kingdom of heaven is like a farmer who went out to hire workers to work in the vineyard. He hired workers at nine in the morning and promised them a fair wage. He did the same to groups of workers at noon, at 3:00 p.m., and finally at 5:00 p.m. But when it came time to pay the workers, he paid them all the same amount. As I expect I would have done, the workers who worked all day had a hissy fit. Why should the guys who only worked a fraction of the time get paid the same as the guys who worked all day?

The landowner defends his actions because the agreement he had with the earlier hires was fair in their eyes when they were hired.

> But he answered one of them, "I am not being unfair to you, friend. Didn't you agree to work for a denarius? Take your pay and go. I want to give the one who was hired last the same as I gave you. Don't I have the right to do what I want with my own money? Or are you envious because I am generous?" *(Matthew 20:13–15)*

Aside from the important lesson about heaven, the parable illustrates the human tendency to be happy with our lot until we have the rude realization that someone else got better treatment than we did.

That story was always tough for me to hear, but I was seriously convicted when I read the exchange between Peter and Jesus at the end of John 21. On the heels of Jesus's compassionate response to Peter's betrayal, culminating with Jesus's description of how Peter's death will glorify God and his command to Peter to follow him, Peter should have been filled with such humility and awe that he could do little more than stand and stammer. But probably because he was human, Peter sees John, goes down the path to comparing himself, and says, "Lord, what about him?" Jesus is pretty frank in his response. "If I want him to remain alive until I return, what is that to you? You must follow me" (John 21:22).

That story stops me in my tracks. If I ever hear Jesus say to me, "What is that to you?", I anticipate that I will feel appropriately reprimanded. If there is ever a phrase to cause me to revisit and promptly suspend my tendency to compare myself to others, I'm thinking that might be it.

A New Yardstick

Rather than looking externally for a measurement, we have the opportunity to focus on our own work. Paul makes that point to the Galatians when he encourages them to carry one another's burdens, check their attitudes, and do good to others. "Each one should test their own actions. Then they can take pride in themselves alone, without comparing themselves to someone else, for each one should carry their own load" (Galatians 6:4–5).

The New American Standard Bible translates the phrase as "each one must examine his own work." Our work can be the gauge by which we measure our progress individually, rather than contrasting it with others.

While I certainly have felt discouraged at times by the work towering over me, I also have found times of joy doing my job. It generally happens when the task I am doing is fulfilling, creative, and aligns with my skills. I'm energized when the quality of my work is good, when I have worked really hard and produced a really good result. There is great fulfillment in using the gifts we are given in the world of work. It is an opportunity to be in the "zone," doing what we were made to do. It's at those times when I connect with the concept of work as a form of worship. My prayer is that everyone finds those opportunities in their workdays.

Work to Serve Others

I also feel it when I can see, or at least imagine, how the work I'm doing will benefit the person at the end of the transaction. I have always found that work becomes more gratifying the more I can connect it to the people who benefit from my labor. Seeing how the communications I produce helps a customer better navigate her interactions with my company, for instance, is a small way that I have made things better for her. I'm sometimes kind of taken aback when I see that happen, because it's easy to forget how our work impacts others when we get caught up in the day-to-day routine.

But I also have to make sure I don't fall for the false benefit of others' praise. Doing work that is intrinsically valuable provides a benefit inherent in the work, a natural product of applying my skills to produce quality work. That's a different measure of performance than counting the volume of praise people give me for my work. Don't get me wrong, I get a rush when someone compliments my work. But I also recognize that the reward of praise appeals to my ego. It can distort my view of myself. And it just perpetuates that tendency I have to compare myself to others. "I can't help but notice that I got praised. What did you get?"

Satisfied Where We Are

There's another state of mind that tamps down my tendency to compare myself to others. It's elusive for me, but very pleasing when I capture it. It's called *contentment*.

Contentment is yet another concept I don't think is part of the typical MBA track. I think of it as finding peace or satisfaction with your current state. It's a rare thing in our world. Achieving contentment may not be possible on our own. It requires relying on a preeminent relationship with Jesus to realign the priorities of your current situation and feel satisfied. The word I like even better is *fulfilled*. When I imagine being fulfilled, I imagine all the space I have for desires filled full with something that doesn't wear out, run out, or get lost.

While I think it requires holy help to find contentment, there are things we can do to help spur it along. The first is to stop consciously checking to see what others have. Maybe that's stepping back from social media, or over-the-top television shows or videos that highlight a lifestyle no one really needs. I've gotten better at that as I learn to recognize that all people have different priorities and interests. Comparing myself to them is just not useful.

The second technique to foster contentment is to practice gratitude. Yes, there are a lot of things I don't have. But there are also a lot of things I do have, both material and nonmaterial: relationships, abilities, circumstances. Shifting my focus to the blessings I have helps prevent my tendency to look around to see what others have that I might want. It may seem silly to stop and list the blessings I have received, but it is a powerful reminder to see how much there is on the list.

A third element of fostering contentment is forcing myself to look beyond my superficial interactions with others to see the full view of their lives. Instead of looking at what they have or where their careers are going, it helps to truly engage with others. It doesn't take long to see that they are facing challenges, setbacks, and frustrations that may be the same, may be less, or may be more than what I'm dealing with. As we see others as fellow travelers who also need the Good News in their lives, perhaps it will reduce the feeling we have to outrun them to grab what we don't have.

There's an internet meme I really relish at this stage in my life. Rather than struggle with FOMO, the Fear of Missing Out, I'm drawn to JOMO, the Joy of Missing Out. It's feeling content with laying low and disconnecting rather than being afraid to miss something. I love the idea of getting as much of a dopamine rush from *not* rushing after something as I would from pursuing something.

The author of Hebrews reminds his readers that we have a treasure that doesn't require us to run or strive or worry. "Keep your lives free from the love of money and be content with what you have, because God has said, 'Never will I leave you; never will I forsake you'" (Hebrews 13:5).

My wise grandmother had it right when she said, "A true blessing is not having what you want, but wanting what you have."

Of course, that was easy for her to say.

She drove a sports car.

CHAPTER 12:

Communicating Gooder

Based on my resume, you might assume that I am good at communicating. After all, I have spent years wrestling gobs of words out of thin air to force them onto paper and, more recently, onto digital screens. I have semesters of education and a couple pieces of high-quality paper that indicate I've been trained to communicate good, er, well. I could even make the case that I am a professional communicator. (As long as you use "professional" not to ascribe some standard of quality to my work product but to simply mean that organizations have given me money to do communicating-type things for them. That sets me apart from all the amateur communicators I work with. Or, uh, whom with I work.)

I would even go so far to say that I was something of a communications prodigy. I'm not sure when children begin talking, but the way I remember it, I was way ahead of everyone else. I was using full words in elementary school and began forming complete sentences while I was in high school. (But I only did that with my friends. My parents maintain that communications with them during my high school years remained, "NO!" and "MINE!" and "WAAAAAHH!")

Communicating at Work

With that sterling vitae, I should be an effective communicator in the workplace. Unfortunately, that is not the case. My workplace communications wayfaring is littered with missteps, mis-speaks, and mistypes. Several examples are the stuff of lore at my employers:

- I once misplaced the location of a decimal point—a teeny, tiny decimal point, barely even noticeable—on a slide in the CEO's annual meeting speech. In doing that, I assisted the CEO in communicating to investors that their quarterly dividend payout would be one-tenth of what they were anticipating. The reaction was swift. I still feel bad for the nursing home full of investors who panicked and sold their stock. I took some consolation knowing they would have something interesting to talk about over meals for weeks to come.

- While emceeing a company-wide leadership meeting, I began the day with a series of slides showing the covers of popular leadership books. I had altered the titles to be hysterically funny and superimposed a photo of my face on every book cover. Apparently, the leadership team was not as entertained as I was. I received the lowest ratings on the evaluation form sent around after the meeting. I'm certain other presenters would have gotten equally bad marks, but my opening caused most of the attendees to walk out during the meeting's first thirty minutes. If participants had just stayed for the second half hour of my slides, I bet my evaluation would have improved dramatically.

- I gushingly shared with an employee the good news that Lisa was hired to the manager position, and wouldn't it be great to finally have someone competent in that role? I forgot that the employee to whom I was speaking had also applied for the job and had been doing it on an interim basis for the past three months. I was reminded of those facts when she burst into tears.

Scriptural Authority of Communications

As if my own experiences weren't enough to document my communications shortcomings, I also don't measure up to the biblical examples of how to communicate well. Tracking my gaps as kind of a checklist for ineffective communications, I can check every box—sometimes all within a single meeting.

- I don't use the best language, especially when I don't get my way. "But now you must also rid yourselves of all such things as these: anger, rage, malice, slander, and filthy language from your lips" (Colossians 3:8).
- I talk more than I listen. "My dear brothers and sisters, take note of this: Everyone should be quick to listen, slow to speak and slow to become angry" (James 1:19).
- I talk without thinking. "Those who consider themselves religious and yet do not keep a tight rein on their tongues deceive themselves, and their religion is worthless" (James 1:26).

- I come across as thinking I'm better than other people. "They pour out arrogant words; all the evildoers are full of boasting" (Psalm 94:4).
- I am sometimes less than honest. "So stop telling lies. Let us tell our neighbors the truth, for we are all parts of the same body" (Ephesians 4:25, NLT).
- I say things that actually make my relationships worse. "So get rid of all evil behavior. Be done with all deceit, hypocrisy, jealousy, and all unkind speech" (1 Peter 2:1, NLT).
- I sometimes fall into what we euphemistically call "corporate speak" to make sure that it's so confusing people can't figure out who is at fault or what the problem is. "Above all, my brothers and sisters, do not swear—not by heaven or by earth or by anything else. All you need to say is a simple 'Yes' or 'No.' Otherwise you will be condemned" (James 5:12).
- My mouth sometimes leads me into sin. "Do not let your mouth lead you into sin" (Ecclesiastes 5:6).
- I gush folly. "The tongue of the wise adorns knowledge, but the mouth of the fool gushes folly" (Proverbs 15:2).

Speaking without Commitment

There's another communications sin I commit frequently. I spend a phenomenal amount of time talking about stuff that doesn't matter. "But avoid worldly and empty chatter, for it will lead to further ungodliness" (2 Timothy 2:16, NASB). A lot of times that manifests as small talk. Most of us don't really seek the opportunity to make small talk, but we all do it, especially if you work where there is more than one other person. Small talk is usually the minimal level of politeness—a way of acknowledging the other person without really establishing a relationship with that person.

I have my own small talk system I use when I want to be pleasant but am not inclined to commit to a full conversation.

Me: "Hey. How's it going?"
Them: "Good. You?"
Me: "Good."

If I have done it correctly, by now we are already moving on in opposite directions. But we are able to go our separate ways, unencumbered, secure in knowing that our relationship is still in a good place. We will be able to pick up right where we left off, whether we see each other later in the day or two years from now. And when we meet again, we'll undoubtedly repeat the identical exchange.

I have another coworker who relishes small talk. For him, it's a game. Consequently, I try to run or get the elevator door to close quickly when "Chatty Carl" is headed my way. An example of Carl's greatest hits:

"Hot enough for you?" For those of you who make a living herding sheep and don't have anyone to talk to all day, this is a surefire small talk-starter. In this case, however, we were in Minneapolis. In January. It was 12 below outside.

I decided to minimize the interaction by stating the obvious.
"It's cold outside!"
"Yeah," he snickered, "but it's a dry cold!" He volleyed on. "Staying busy?"
"Uh-huh. And you?" (It's rude not to return the question.)
"Can't complain; no one listens to me anyway!" He giggled. "See the game last night?"
"Uh-uh."

"Yeah, it's a shame they traded [insert player's name here]. If I didn't have such a bum arm, I'd tell [insert coach's name here] to put me in. But I'd have to take a pay cut." Followed again by that self-entertaining laughter that's only funny when I do it.

Recently, I decided I was done with small talk. I wasn't going to miss one more opportunity to speak eternal truth when I saw someone I knew. I began by launching into discussions of Christian doctrines. ("So, Audrey, don't you think the Transfiguration of Jesus really represents the connecting point between the temporal and the eternal?")

But that didn't go over well, either. Apparently, such an exchange is a bit off-putting for people, probably because it reveals their embarrassing lack of deep faith. Or maybe they just prefer small talk.

There's Hope for Me Yet

Despite all of that, I keep trying to communicate. Mostly because I don't really have a choice not to. My communications at work may leave a lot to be desired, but it would be even worse—and just plain awkward—if I stopped trying.

I'd like to think I'm getting better. I'd like to think the older I get and the more I shift my focus from myself to God, the more careful I am with what I say. It helps to spend time reading Scripture. The purpose of Scripture is not to make me feel guilty for my failings, but to provide guidance for right living. And Scripture includes a boatload of guidance on how to communicate. The above list just scratches the surface. There are hundreds of references to communications in the Old and New Testaments. If you don't believe me, you should read the Bible this evening and count how many times you see the words *speak*, or *talk*, or even *grumble*. I bet you will lose count.

When I did that last night, I had an interesting realization. (OK, I'm exaggerating. It took me two nights to read the Bible. Although it wasn't the "real" Bible—it was the *Big Bible Picture Book for Kids*. But it still had a lot of good stuff in it.)

Two things struck me. First, I tend to think of communication as one person (usually me) speaking or talking or grumbling. I sometimes forget that communication generally involves at least two people. It's the way we exchange not just information, but also what we feel—from love to fear, from encouragement to anger. On the surface, it may be words passing between the talker and the listener. But what's really going on is connection and relationship.

Second, if communicating is connecting, then what we do in that space is pretty important. And here's where I think Scripture has a vital message for anyone who communicates. The opportunity to communicate is not to just exchange information but to build up one another.

Why We Speak

There's a passage in Paul's letter to Ephesians where I feel like this all comes together. In a portion of his letter that provides instructions for Christian living, Paul talks about both what people should say and why it is important. We are to use our communications to promote kindness and compassion, sharing words that are wholesome and free of any underlying anger or bitterness. We communicate because it builds others up, eases their burdens, and paints for them a picture of God's amazing grace.

Do not let any unwholesome talk come out of your mouths, but only what is helpful for building others up according to their needs, that it may benefit those who listen. And do not grieve the Holy Spirit of God, with whom you were sealed for the day of redemption. Get rid of all bitterness, rage and anger, brawling and slander, along with every form of malice. Be kind and compassionate to one another, forgiving each other, just as in Christ God forgave you. *(Ephesians 4:29–32)*

This passage gives our routine daily interactions an oversized value in building relationships. As Christians, we are called to use the opportunity we have with coworkers, colleagues, and customers to be a force for positive interactions, to minister to and point people toward a better way of living and adoption into God's family.

At least that's what I got out of it. But I gush folly, so I might not be the best one to listen to.

Or who to listen to whom.

CHAPTER 13

The Perils of Ownership

My colleague Quentin (not his real name, but a *nom de work*, to protect his identity in the unflattering story I'm about to tell) was a department head at the company where I worked. After a series of promotions, Quentin awoke one day to find himself in charge of an entire department. He oversaw a budget of several million dollars and a staff of more than thirty people.

Quentin took this good fortune personally. He let everyone know about his esteemed place in the organization. Whenever he was in a meeting, he would invariably say something like, "I'll get my team to work on that," or "I told my team that wasn't going to fly"—or, the most annoying, "I'll have my people take a look at that and get back to you."

We've all heard the throwaway line, "Have your people call my people." But Quentin meant it. He said it so often that we all rolled our eyes whenever he did. I often had this image of a bunch of Little Leaguers with "Quentin's Team" across the back of their uniforms. Or maybe a dungeon where Quentin kept "his team" bound to computer desks. Neither visual did much to elevate Quentin's professional standing in my mind. Nor apparently in someone else's mind because, for whatever reason, Quentin was first demoted and then left the company "to pursue other teams."

Taking What Isn't Yours

I feel a twinge of sadness when I hear someone say something like "my team." It's particularly unnerving when I catch myself saying it. I'm worried that the speaker is taking credit for something that God actually owns. Whenever someone asserts complete possession of a department, a team, or a project, I call this an Ownership Issue. It's an issue because that person thinks he or she owns something he or she doesn't. (In law enforcement circles, I believe that's called "burglary.")

A blatant example occurred at a company holiday party. One of the senior executives hosting the event asserted several times that he had made the event possible. (I believe his exact words upon greeting employees were, "Thanks for coming; I made this possible.") He indicated that he had provided the wonderful food, the fine facility, and the bountiful beverages.

By asserting ownership, the executive probably made himself feel important and convinced himself that he was capable of great generosity for an employee event. That was ironic, however, because generosity had nothing to do with it. The party cost him nothing personally. It was paid for out of the company budget, and his administrative assistant did all the work. At the very least, he should have credited her for hiring the caterer, reserving the hall, and processing the invoices. Mr. Senior Executive probably didn't even sign the invoice pay authorization.

Accumulation Syndrome

I'm not sure what the root cause of this assertion of ownership is (although that won't prevent me from speculating about it). I suspect it arises out of a natural (i.e., worldly) sense of fear or insecurity. Perhaps it is borne from a desire for people to feel better about themselves. But rather than turn to God for our security, we turn to stuff, and we get possessive.

We can get possessive when it comes to inanimate objects like offices, desk chairs, and favorite staplers. We can also try to own people. I have seen managers take great price in the number of boxes on the org chart that report to them. My friend Quentin was able to drop into casual conversation that he had a staff of thirty-two people. As sordid as it was, you had to admire his skill in working that fact into conversation so effortlessly.

Even if we don't supervise people, we have to ask ourselves if we try to keep friends and coworkers to ourselves. Are we jealous if they choose to go to lunch with someone else or meet up with another group after work? Whose team are they on, anyway?

I expect that entrepreneurs are particularly susceptible to this possessive behavior. Most of us came into a company that existed before we were hired. We probably even recognize that chances are good the company will exist after we're gone. But if you are a company founder, it's particularly easy to fall into the "I did this" trap. After all, before you came, there was vast nothingness. After you arrived, greatness. How can anyone not see the amazing impact you had?

Crediting the True Power and Strength

It's important to have a sense of responsibility for the things we are responsible for. God is all about following through on what he said and keeping his covenant. The danger comes when we credit our own efforts and forget that God had a role in the outcome. Again, Deuteronomy 8:17–19 speaks directly to the danger of this possession attitude:

> You may say to yourself, "My power and the strength of my hands have produced this wealth for me." But remember the LORD your God, for it is He who gives you the ability to produce wealth. . . . If you ever forget the LORD your God and follow other gods and worship and bow down to them, I testify against you today that you will surely be destroyed.

Being a Good Steward

Scripture provides an effective vaccination against the outbreak of excessive ownership fever. It is the concept of stewardship.

Stewardship means you are a caretaker for something. You manage something with the proper regard for the rights of others. As the steward, you have responsibility for the item or property, but you don't own it. It's your job, however, to see that the item is well managed and fruitful.

In Christian circles, we usually talk about stewardship when fundraising or when annual pledge time rolls around. The whole point is to get us to stop being so tightfisted with the money God has provided us, since it's not ours, anyway.

Peter makes it plain that the gifting we have received is meant to be shared for others' benefit when he writes, "Each of you should use whatever gift you have received to serve others, as faithful stewards of God's grace in its various forms" (1 Peter 4:10).

Stewardship Begins at Home

Stewardship has applications for people, too. Start with family members. I don't own my wife, but as the man in the family, I am expected to love her, cherish her, and present her to Jesus at the end day as perfect and unsoiled as she was when he created her. (That's "unsoiled," not "unspoiled." My wife points out she would be perfectly happy being spoiled with expensive gifts and, even better, a long list of completed household chores.)

I also don't get to own my children—they belong to God—but he has granted me the opportunity to raise them, teach them, and care for them while they are in this world. He'll get them back someday, and I'll be held accountable for what shape they're in when they show up on his doorstep. (Fortunately, I had the foresight to sign up for the insurance policy with the exclusion for skinned knees and elbows.)

Stewardship also works very nicely when applied to our jobs. It's easy to feel a sense of ownership for something you labor over all day. If I am a department head, I can believe that I own the people, the budget, and the output from "my" department. But if I were no longer here, the company would replace me. I no more "own" the department than I "own" the concrete space where I park my car every day. When the nice security guard escorts me out the front door (which is only a matter of time, at the rate I'm going), it's not as if I'll be packing my parking space into the cardboard box to take home with me. We should see most of our work that way.

When you see yourself as a steward of the department, the team, or the job, you feel a sense of responsibility—regarding the needs of others—without the sense of ownership entitlement. You can appreciate that you're acting on behalf of the ultimate owner—God. Just as I need to do with my family, I'd better be able to turn the department, the staff, and the work over to the next caretaker in better condition than I found them. As much as I might like to think I own them, they will move to someone else's care when I move on.

Just ask Quentin. "His" team is doing just fine without him, thank you.

CHAPTER 14:

The Problem of Pride

U p until now, this book has been all fun and games. We've shared some laughs, read a little Scripture, and affirmed that I'm bad at both work and living out my faith. It's been a hoot.

But that's about to change. It's time we get serious and address one of the most destructive practices that can quash our ability to live out our faith at work. It's the great barrier to holiness, the major obstacle to living a life focused on Jesus. I'm talking about the pinnacle of the seven deadly sins: pride.

Pride is a big obstacle to faith because it orients your world around *you*. Not Jesus, not your family, not even Thursday Night Football. It makes everything about you. That's kind of the antithesis of living out your faith. It's hard to demonstrate care and concern for others when you're always worried about how caring for others cuts into your "me" time. Related to that is a lack of gratefulness for any good thing God or anyone else did for you, because it was undoubtedly your own skills, or smarts, or "natural abilities" that accomplished all that you accomplished. (Don't ask me how I know this. That's not important right now. Pay attention.)

Maybe I shouldn't assume that you struggle with pride. Maybe pride isn't the issue for you that it is for me. Maybe you have a track record of walking in grace and don't need an extra-long chapter on pride. If that's the case, good for you! Perhaps you would be so kind as to contact me at your earliest convenience and tell me how you've managed to keep your pride in check. Perhaps you should be writing this chapter when this book undoubtedly goes back for one of its many reprint runs. But for now, there's only one printing, and since pride is one of my greatest struggles, you can just sit here and struggle with me.

A Primer on Pride

The word *pride* gets thrown around so much these days that it can be easy to dismiss it as unimportant. So it's worthwhile to stop and think about it for a moment. I don't have to go much further than reading the dictionary definitions of pride to be reminded of the damage pride can do. For instance, there's "a high or inordinate opinion of one's own dignity, importance, merit, or superiority." (I wince at the definition of *inordinate*: "not within proper or reasonable limits, immoderate, excessive.") The other definition that I like/hate to think applies to me is as follows: "Pride is an excessive view of oneself without regard for others." Or, if that seems too harsh, pride can be "a feeling of deep pleasure or satisfaction derived from one's own achievements." That doesn't make it sound quite as toxic.

Regardless of how you define it, pride can distort our relationship to God. Our pastor said that when we get prideful, we tend to make God small. When we believe we are solely responsible for our successes, through our abilities or sheer effort, we fail to recognize the role of God and his blessings. Not submitting our mind to God means we can legitimize our behavior because we feel we alone accomplished this great thing. (At least that's what my pastor said. Although it sounds right.)

What's the big deal? you may be thinking, undoubtedly trying to justify your own prideful behavior. *We should be proud of our accomplishments. They were God-given, right? Shouldn't we celebrate them?*

I get it. I'm with you. I also spend an inordinate amount of time trying to justify my own prideful behavior. But Scripture doesn't paint human pride in a very positive light. Cain gave us a lovely example in the book of Genesis of how not to let your pride get the better of you. Moses spent a lot of time in Deuteronomy trying to educate the Israelites about pride. He encouraged them not to forget God by failing to observe God's commands, laws, and decrees.

> Otherwise, when you eat and are satisfied, when you build fine houses and settle down, and when your herds and flocks grow large and your silver and gold increase and all you have is multiplied, then your heart will become proud and you will forget the LORD your God, who brought you out of Egypt, out of the land of slavery. *(Deuteronomy 8:12–14)*

Psalms and Proverbs also seem really down on pride. Consider Proverbs 16:5, for instance: "The LORD detests all the proud of heart. Be sure of this: They will not go unpunished." Or Proverbs 3:34: "He mocks proud mockers but shows favor to the humble and oppressed."

And it's not just a concept only discussed in the Old Testament. The New Testament has plenty of rebukes of pride and prideful behavior. Like Paul's letter to the Romans: "Live in harmony with each other. Don't be too proud to enjoy the company of ordinary people. And don't think you know it all!" (Romans 12:16, NLT). Or his first letter to Timothy: "Teach those who are rich in this world not to be proud and not to trust in their money, which is so unreliable. Their trust should be in God, who richly gives us all we need for our enjoyment" (1 Timothy 6:17, NLT). And then there's the great love chapter in Paul's letter to the Corinthians: "Love is patient and kind. Love is not jealous or boastful or proud" (1 Corinthians 13:4, NLT).

Pride at Work

We can struggle with pride in lots of areas of our lives, but it's a real challenge in the workplace. The business world spends a lot of time telling us we need to be aggressive and assertive; we need to make things happen and get results. We've got deadlines, quotas, and goals to meet. And when we meet them, we are rewarded with promotions and salary increases and other good things. There's no room on that agenda for being contemplative, reflective, and listening to determine what would please your Creator. In Christian circles, *long-term* means eternity. In business circles, *long-term* means the end of the day—but more likely the end of the meeting you're sitting in right now.

The work world incents us to be productive, be successful, be competitive, and achieve great things. And when we do, and we accumulate those rewards, it's easy to develop a firm and strident belief that we accomplished it all on our own. Solo. Singly. Sans assistance. Me, Myself, and Moi. Pride is a brash and abrasive boast that we are smarter, more successful, and more deserving than our colleagues, who are now just so many rungs on the ladder we've successfully climbed.

I'm pretty sure that's the wrong response. But in the work world, you see it all the time. Colleagues, clients, and coworkers get all pumped up with pride about something "they" did. It's quite unappealing when you see a coworker—who, a moment ago, was nice, steady, and normal—get proud and boastful when she gets a promotion or a big project to lead. Even if she already feels superior to everyone in the office, when something good happens she thinks she accomplished on her own, her overdeveloped ego grows to menacing proportions.

It's sort of like a 1950s black-and-white science fiction movie. The ego continues to grow until it's bursting out of the windows of the building, threatening the city by the bay. The army tries to stop it, but their puny guns are useless. It's up to the misunderstood hero and the nerdy but beautiful (or handsome) scientist to try to stop the giant ego from taking over the entire world.

Well, you get the idea.

We get into trouble when we leave the path of modesty and wander onto the busy thoroughfare of "I did this." It's a perilous place to be. It's disorienting and dangerous. You can get injured there.

Maintaining Pride Momentum

If we know pride is a problem, and Scripture tells us we shouldn't take credit for God's works, why do we keep doing it? At the risk of projecting my own insecurities on the entire human population, I think it's another case of trying to compensate for all the things that beat down our self-esteem. Our egos want to take credit for any good that we do. We're starved for recognition and affirmation, so when we do something positive, we want to take credit for it, and we want to give others not credit, but the opportunity to celebrate us. It may feel natural, but it's not God's desire for us. "God is opposed to the proud but gives grace to the humble" (James 4:6, NLT).

If we're looking for a reason to feel good about ourselves, we should start with the fact that we are beloved sons or daughters of the most high God, who seeks us out for an eternity of fellowship with him. But that's usually not enough for us ungrateful children. (Again, sorry if I'm projecting here.) Instead, we try to grab a piece of something in this world and hold on to it as our very own.

Value of Humility

Fortunately, God gave us substitute for the menacing pride monster. It's called humility. Humility is the practice of setting aside our own independence, submitting ourselves to God, and giving him the appropriate credit for the good he has done.

If you work in a corporation, it's quite possible you may not be familiar with the concept of humility. Humility is not something that's generally encouraged or modeled at work. I don't believe humility is a subject they teach at the finest business schools. In fact, I wouldn't be surprised if they instead offered courses on "How to Think More Highly of Yourself Than You Ought." (There must be such a program. I know I've met some successful honors graduates.)

But we don't need a class on this topic. Jesus gave us the ultimate example of humility. He modeled selflessness, compassion, and an abiding focus on others more than himself. He demonstrated that the key to achieving humility begins with submission. We just need to follow his lead. Simply submit your dreams, desires, and your will to God, and you're home free! That's all there is to it! What's the problem?

The problem is that I am a weak, selfish creature who doesn't like to look weak and selfish. So I pretend I have it all together. I tell myself and others that I really am doing great things, making a difference, and worth every penny they pay me. Actually, I'm worth a lot more than what they pay me! If it wasn't for me, this place would be nowhere! I rock!

Paul faced the temptation to say, "I rock," but God provided a humbling experience that prevented him from getting too caught up in himself. As he wrote:

> For this reason, to keep me from exalting myself, there was given me a thorn in the flesh, a messenger of Satan to torment me—to keep me from exalting myself! Concerning this I implored the Lord three times that it might leave me. And He has said to me, "My grace is sufficient for you, for power is perfected in weakness." Most gladly, therefore, I will rather boast about my weaknesses, so that the power of Christ may dwell in me. *(2 Corinthians 12:7–9, NASB)*

Good for you, Paul, but I'm not too keen on that. Exalting in weakness? Give me a break! If the guys at the office knew I was weak, they'd eat me for lunch. They wouldn't respect me. They wouldn't let me sit at the cool table. (Work really is a lot like high school.)

But here's the real joke. We're all weak. We're all hiding behind masks of hurts and confusion and loneliness and sadness. Or as author Peggy Noonan wrote, quoting a TSA agent who has seen it all, "Everyone's carrying the same things."[4] We're undoubtedly carrying the same toothpaste, deodorant, and Hanes underwear.

But I like the metaphorical interpretation that we're all carrying hurts, anger, frustration, loneliness . . . the list goes on and on. Even worse, although we're carrying all that, we're all acting like it's cool. Is it any wonder we're stressed out at work? If you think humility is hard work, stop and think how much energy you're spending trying to pretend you're perfect. Wouldn't it be easier if we just let people see our weaker side and trust God to use that openness to touch other people's hearts? Vulnerability is a powerful stance to adopt if you want to connect with others. (But you go first, just in case.)

Achieving Humility by Force

At some point, you may decide to step off the stage, set aside the mask, and go all in on humility. I heard a speaker once say that we must begin by making a conscious decision if we want to achieve humility. Then we must continually submit our spirit and will to God's authority. That seems like higher-level thinking to me. I, on the other hand, through years of practice and experience, have developed a multistep program guaranteed to generate humility when it's not present. It is a cycle I have repeated so many times, I am able to recite it without consulting my notes.

Step one on the path to humility begins, ironically enough, with success. I do something well at work. I may have directed a project or prepared a memo that allows my organization to advance toward its goals. When I do that, I am rightly recognized for my significant, life-changing contribution and lauded for my excellent work. In response, rather than give thanks to the Giver of All Good Things, I take a different route. I grow proud.

Step two is to find myself in a situation, fresh from my recent triumph, where my help might be needed on something. Flush with my superior contribution in the last effort, I anticipate everyone will be eager for my thoughts and my contribution. I render my assistance or my wise opinion. Yet the crowds do not fall prostrate to my brilliance. In fact, they continue talking and discussing, *almost as if I hadn't spoken!* But how can this be? My wisdom is equal to or even greater to what I exhibited earlier. Confused but undaunted, I wait for another opportunity to express my acumen. The opportunity invariably comes, and I again proffer wisdom, yet there is the same lack of response.

If I were to choose a spiritually mature response, I would gratefully read the signs and recognize I need to change course. But I don't do that. Instead, I turn inward, ramping up the self-talk that assures me I am "right" and everyone else is "wrong." Expecting to see foolish behavior, I see it in abundance. I grow so self-righteous I can barely understand why I even bother trying to work with these silly, simple people.

The process culminates with me taking some action or saying something that produces a stunning fall. I essentially achieve humility by force. I may gossip to someone about the lack of skills of the team members, only to have word of my hurtful comments get back to the team members. I may sniff in a meeting that "their" solution is clearly folly, such that everyone in the meeting looks at me blankly, recognizing the cluelessness in myself that I haven't yet identified.

Way too late in the process, I finally realize that pride and self-will have not served me well. I've damaged relationships, losing (or reinforcing that I never had) the trust and respect of my peers. And I have fallen so far from the standard that Jesus set for his followers. I still reached Humble City, but I took the long way there and arrived broken and bruised.

Working My Way Back

For those who don't want to take my long and winding path to humility, there is a route to the same destination that won't break relationships or hurt feelings. Here are a few techniques that can save you a lot of trouble.

Pray. It's a recurring theme—I can't successfully fight my sinful nature on my own. I need holy power to get through it. I have to ask God to help me remember and model humility. Paul tells us in Romans 12:3 not to think more highly of ourselves than we ought to think. In Philippians 2:3, he tells us to regard one another as more important than ourselves. The only way I've found to sincerely do that is to ask for God's help.

Give thanks. Practicing gratitude is a great way to embrace humility. When I tally up all the stuff, relationships, and circumstances God has provided for me, I can't help but be humbled by God's generosity and my own undeservedness.

Do good works for others. By helping others, I am reminded of how we are dependent upon one another. Helping others allows me to see that I can change people's lives for the better. Doing good works for others can also be a path to pride, however, if I'm not careful. Helping others for my own benefit or to create indebtedness to me isn't helping. That's why I like the next one as a variation.

Do good works for others anonymously. When I minister to someone so only God knows it was me doing the work, I can be humbled by the simple practice of helping someone in need with no ability to be rewarded (at least in this life).

Let others do good works for you. Allowing others to help you, however, is the true test of humility. I struggle with this one big-time. After all, I am a grown-up. I have a good job. I (and the bank) own a home and two cars. I am perfectly capable of taking care of myself. The idea that I would rely on someone else for assistance is very, very hard for me. So why would I do that? Because God designed us to be interdependent, connected, and willing to help one another. By putting myself in a position to be helped by others, I can accept grace and not see it as my own doing. "Let us then approach God's throne of grace with confidence, so that we may receive mercy and find grace to help us in our time of need" (Hebrews 4:16).

Get perspective. Broadening your perspective is a great way to achieve a sense of humility, and it can be done in a number of pleasant ways. Comfort someone who is facing a tough time. Spend time with an older person or with kids. Go someplace where you can experience natural beauty. These are all ways to get off the workplace merry-go-round and be reminded of what's really important.

My wife is a cancer survivor. Following her successful treatment, every year her group of cancer survivor cohorts had a dinner to celebrate another year of life. I was always embarrassed when I walked into that event preoccupied by whatever little problem was troubling me at the moment. Nothing puts the little annoyances of a bad day in perspective like being around people who are rejoicing to be alive.

Connect with people. Because I don't like strangers, and I assume they are out to hurt me or take my things (I really do have some serious issues), I am always humbled by how nice people can be once I get to know them. Maybe it's a result of having undesirably low expectations of people, but I am so often taken aback at how seldom people do seem to want to hurt me. (Although there are always exceptions—notably among the people who know me well.)

The strongest connection occurs when I commit to develop a real, intimate relationship with an individual or a group. That's why churches love small groups. The New Testament church used small groups or home churches for a reason. When I spend regular time with a small group, and we share the joys and sorrows of our lives, I develop a serious case of compassion. It's humbling when someone allows you into their lives that deeply.

Read the great Christian authors. I also find reading a good foundational book to be a good way to build humility. There is nothing like reading the great Christian authors like C.S. Lewis, J.I. Packer, or my favorite modern Christian writer, Richard Foster, to be humbled by their ability to capture the essence of God and faith in such touching and practical terms. Reading those authors, I feel a tiny sense of connection with them and a thought that just maybe I can change my thinking to be more aligned with their wisdom. After all, I worship the very same God they do!

Finding Humility, One Way or Another

Even if you aren't looking for it, humility can sometimes find you. I find it when I practice my humanity and make a mistake. I don't plan for it, but it happens. I reach for God's grace and begin my climb toward a contrite heart, a humble spirit, and a grateful response. It's always important to remember that you are valued simply as a child of God. Your identity is so well established by his claim on you that you are priceless. When you reflect on his love and compassion for you, well, that in itself is a humbling experience.

Or, if that doesn't work, put yourself in the position of the Galatians when Paul exhorted them to help one another. "If you think you are too important to help someone, you are only fooling yourself. You are not that important" (Galatians 6:3, NLT).

Nothing like a rejoinder from Paul to help you feel humble. But don't be so prideful to think he was only talking to you. This was a long chapter, and you don't want to have to reread it.

CHAPTER 15

Talking Myself into Being Important

As if the last chapter on pride wasn't enough, here comes another one. Except this chapter is focused on one particularly annoying way I—uh, *we*—show our pride at work.

Perhaps this has happened to you. You are talking to a colleague about some work topic. You are both knowledgeable about the topic and have perspectives on how to address it. Yet, if you really listen, you and your colleague aren't talking about the issue at all. You're actually talking about yourselves.

Now, to someone overhearing your conversation, it sounds productive. But if you chart it out, you can see the oh-so-subtle ways each person manages to work into the conversation a focus on himself or herself.

Here's an actual conversation I had with a colleague recently that illustrates my point.

She: "I don't know, I don't think it makes a lot of sense to spend the money on this sponsorship. I'm not convinced it will reach the audience we're trying to reach."

Me: "I know. I thought the same thing about the time I sponsored the Olympics. I had my doubts, but it really was an awesome time. Rio de Janeiro was amazing, and I got to meet a lot of incredible athletes. As I said to Simone Biles and Michael Phelps . . ."

She: "I'm sure. But this isn't quite the same. I think two thousand dollars to sponsor the webinar series is pricey, especially if we don't know who's watching."

Me: "Yep. I thought the same thing when I sponsored the Academy Awards. Viewership wasn't as high as I'd hoped, but it was a real rush being on the red carpet with the cast of *Slumdog Millionaire*. We laughed so hard at . . ."

She: "I'm not convinced. I'll talk to my manager and see what she says."

Me: "Whoa, we get it; you're important! Maybe you could dial the grandstanding back a bit. We're here to work, not showboat!"

That may be an exaggeration (or not). Beyond producing a product or service, I'm convinced that work's primary purpose is to bring together needy people so we can talk about ourselves. I am amazed at how much of my daily work conversations are simply the other person and me saying things that serve only to give us a greater sense of worth. We inject into our work conversations expressions of our value, our experience, and whatever is top of mind. People do this way too much. (And by "people," I mean "I.")

Now, I'm not talking about the legitimate sharing of our stories in a way that builds fellowship and understanding. It's necessary to know about one another's successes and failures, celebrations, and hardships if we are to share with our coworkers and build lasting bonds. I'm talking about the pointless and useless information we work into conversations that serves only to make ourselves feel important.

Work One-upmanship

Work seems to foster this attitude that it's OK to talk about "Me First." I'm not sure how work became this big game of verbal one-upmanship. Maybe it's a result of the constant stresses we feel trying to meet others' expectations. Maybe it's our response to feeling beaten down when work makes us feel small and unappreciated. Maybe we feel compelled to talk about ourselves as winners because work sometimes feels like a competition that produces lots of losers. (Think grade school athletic competitions, but with fewer participation ribbons.)

Whatever reason, people—again, with me at the front of that line—seem to spend a lot of time trying to convince one another that we have value.

Talking About Ourselves

I've noticed many variations on how we do this at work. We can try to deluge the other person through the sheer volume of things we say about ourselves. We can brag about activities we think will impress other people. We share insight into the close relationships we have with executives and important people. We can find ways to talk about our accomplishments even when they don't fit into the conversation we're having.

A colleague of mine was particularly good at this. She served on a national association board for our industry. She could mention that fact several times in a conversation, regardless of our topic.

Me: "I don't know how we're going to make budget this month with the extra expenses and income shortfall."

She: "Well, as you may know, I am Assistant Regional Delegate on the National Trade Association Professional Advisory Board, so why don't I bring this up at our next meeting in Coral Gables to discuss with other board members how they would handle this?"

Me: "Um . . . uh . . . sure."

Subtle Attempts at Substantiation

Even when we try to be subtle about it, our conversations often seem to be about us. Here's a recent example, with the translated "real meaning" of the conversation helpfully provided to make my point.

Me: "Gee, Bob, you look tired."

(*Translation: "Wow, Bob, here I am, standing impatiently in this elevator, late to an incredibly important meeting that probably can't start until I get there. Yet despite that heavy—yet well-placed—*

responsibility, I am still sensitive enough to the needs of the little people around me that I can't help but notice you look tired.")

Bob: "Yeah, it's been a long week."

(Translation: "Not surprisingly, given my incredible commitment and capacity to put others' needs above my own, it is just like me to not even realize how much energy I have expended for the company's benefit. But I guess after spending more than two hundred hours at work these past four days, I should no longer expect to be able to hide the superhuman strain from others.")

Me: "You can say that again!"

(Translation: "Commitment! Hah! What do YOU know about commitment?! I'm so committed to other people that I don't even look tired because it would make them feel uncomfortable, and they'd feel obligated to comment! I guess I win this round, ol' pal!")

Bob: "This is my floor. Take care!"

(Translation: "Don't think for a minute you've won this round, you self-righteous twerp! I'll be back at my desk, completing the mounds of work, while you're spending company time joyriding on the elevator. How will you explain that on your timesheet this week?!")

Me: "See you later!"

(Translation: "Curses! Why didn't I just go to the vending machines on my floor!?")

Valued for Who We Are

While it may just be an annoyance to the rest of the world, I worry that our fixation on talking ourselves up has bigger implications for us Christians—particularly since Scripture is very clear that we don't need to take this approach, given our inherent value to God. In his letter to the Romans, for instance, Paul describes a God who values us so much that the Creator of the universe calls us to himself. "For his Holy Spirit speaks to us deep in our hearts and tells us that we are God's children" (Romans 8:16, NLT). Paul says the same thing in his letter to the Ephesians: "Long ago, even before he made the world, God loved us and chose us in Christ to be holy and without fault in his eyes" (Ephesians 1:4, NLT). And again, in the next chapter: "[God] raised us up with Him, and seated us with Him in the heavenly places in Christ Jesus . . ." (Ephesians 2:6, NASB).

We don't need to talk ourselves up to obtain value that God already has assigned to us. I could talk all day about how important I am. But even my highest opinion of myself would never compare to the significance God has already ascribed to me. I just need to realize that and accept it.

It may be some consolation to know we aren't the first to practice this behavior. The disciples illustrate in an episode in Mark 9 that talking ourselves up doesn't make us more valuable. Jesus catches the disciples arguing about who is the greatest and calls a time-out to explain things. "Sitting down, Jesus called the Twelve and said, 'Anyone who wants to be first must be the very last, and the servant of all'" (Mark 9:35).

In the next chapter, Jesus responds to James and John's request that they be allowed to sit on either side of Jesus when he enters his kingdom. (The story is also told in Matthew 20, with the great twist that it's the mother of James and John who makes the request. Nothing like having Mommy ask if you can have a place of honor. It's so much less awkward than asking yourself.)

> Then James and John, the sons of Zebedee, came to him. "Teacher," they said, "we want you to do for us whatever we ask."
> "What do you want me to do for you?" he asked.
> They replied, "Let one of us sit at your right and the other at your left in your glory." (Mark 10:35–37)

A bit later, Jesus calls the disciples together to explain how the whole "first in line" thing really works in heaven:

> Jesus called them together and said, "You know that those who are regarded as rulers of the Gentiles lord it over them, and their high officials exercise authority over them. Not so with you. Instead, whoever wants to become great among you must be your servant, and whoever wants to be first must be slave of all. For even the Son of Man did not come to be served, but to serve, and to give his life as a ransom for many." *(Mark 10:42–45)*

Thanks to the gawky efforts of the disciples, we have a clear illustration of the desired demeanor to have with others if we accept God's view that we are already of infinite value. We don't need to talk ourselves up to achieve it. It's about submission, mercy, and humility. It's not about finding ways to insert ourselves into the conversation.

(One more note on this story: Acts 12:2 tells how King Herod had James put to death by sword. John went into exile, where he wrote the Book of Revelation. Even these two disciples, who apparently struggled as I often do to understand the vision and words of Jesus, became pillars in our faith, serving up their very lives to advance it. That gives me hope that my puny efforts aren't necessarily the end of the story.)

My Response

Even though I know all this intellectually, I still can't seem to stop talking about myself. I find a way to shift conversations to talk about my victories, my losses, and even how things affect me. How do I change that? Simply being aware of how often I put myself into my conversations would be a good first step. I also pray for a heart turned toward others, rather than focused on my own esteem. I also have asked a trusted friend to help monitor me. Whenever I get going about how central I am to the topic at hand, my friend Don makes a loud, coughing noise and says something like, "Maybe there's another topic we could talk about." To further reinforce it, he makes a slashing motion with his hand at his throat. It's not subtle, but it generally takes un-subtle to get my attention.

Slowly, I'm doing a better job of making conversations more about the other person than about me. With continued progress, I'm even hoping that someday I'll advance to the point where I can share enthusiastically with other people that they, too, are valuable to God.

In full disclosure, this practice is not one I identified on my own. It's a little technique I learned at the Annual Meeting of IAS-FPWWWTHOPR, the International Association of Self-Focused People Who Write Words They Hope Other People Read.

I'm a member, you know.

CHAPTER 16

The Derailing Effect of Expectations

I can list a lot of obstacles that hamper my ability to incorporate faith at work—from selfishness to greed, from gossiping to "borrowing" the company snowplow to clear my driveway. (We got a lot of snow that winter!) But nothing can set me sideways like my misplaced expectations.

Understanding Expectations

Most of us start our workday with some expectation of how our day will go. And even when we say we expect the worst, deep down we think things should go our way. The morning commute should be easy, the video call should function without technology issues, and colleagues should be collegial. Selfishly, I expect things at work to go smoothly. I expect things to work out for me. And sometimes they do. But when work meets my positive expectations, I'm usually not even paying attention. After all, that was what I expected! Of course, that's how my day should go!

It's gotten to the point that I have developed a sense of entitlement about work. I have come to expect that I somehow deserve pleasant outcomes and freedom from any kind of harm, setback, or even inconvenience.

You may be surprised when I tell you that doesn't always happen. (No, seriously!) Sometimes things don't go my way. The project doesn't accomplish what it was intended to accomplish. The customer doesn't sign the contract. I don't get promoted to CEO based on that one particularly well-crafted email.

Things not going the way we expect is the normal course of life. The real problem is my reaction. When my expectations aren't met, my reaction generally is not one of gentle repose and gracious understanding. My reaction tends to be, at best, hours of dramatic whining and, at worst, an outright temper tantrum. Such a reaction often feels appropriate in the moment. But not surprisingly, acting that way tends to hinder my faith walk and undercut my testimony.

It happened to me again recently. Our team project was going well. We had solved some serious issues and had a path to successful completion. The team was unified and excited. We were congratulating ourselves that we had overcome long-standing obstacles (like gravity) to find a workable solution. We had expectations of continued success and future financial rewards. We were about ready to tackle how to get the number of hot dogs and hot dog buns in packages to come out even.

So, we were stunned when the executive sponsor of the project told us that we had a great plan, but it needed to be implemented twice as fast and at half the cost. And it needed to go in the exact opposite direction. It was a setback, and I reacted, as some might characterize, "poorly" (at least that's what the police report said). I had certain expectations that weren't met, and I felt entitled to respond in a way such that everyone knew I wasn't happy about this change. Following that episode, it should come as no surprise that no one sought me out for my wise counsel or asked me to share my faith journey.

Calculating the Expectations

Beginning to realize the extent of my expectations problem, I started categorizing the kinds of expectations I held. I was amazed once I realized how many unrealistic work expectations I had. About the only thing that tied them together was the consistent belief that only good things should happen to me.

Expectations of people: My greatest expectation of people is that they will act in my best interest. I expect my boss to consistently praise my work, my coworkers to drop what they're doing to help me, and the IT help desk person to personally come reboot my computer when I call. It's with great disappointment that I continually learn that other people have their own focus. They are doing their jobs in their own careers. Apparently, these other people are trying to live their own lives—and not in a way that necessarily puts my needs at the forefront. It's very frustrating.

Expectations of rewards: The longer I work, I'm embarrassed to say, the more I think I should be compensated for my work. My salary and my employer perks should climb past the top of the chart. (Don't take my word for it; look it up. It's in the Book of Expectations, Chapter 11.) After all, I bring great longevity and wisdom to my employer the longer I am here. If nothing else, they should pay me more just to keep quiet about the past company failures (which isn't hard, since I've played a significant part in most of them. Which also might explain why my expectation of rewards goes unmet . . .)

Expectations of ease: I have been a productive member of the work world (if you don't get too technical about the definition of *productive*) for a long time. After all that time, I subconsciously think that work should start getting easier. I should be able to simply apply past solutions and not have to solve each new problem anew. "Been there, done that" should translate to "easy street." But like the stock prospectus says, "Past performance is no guarantee of future returns." Or, as one of my coworkers says, "If it was easy, they'd hire monkeys to do it." (I think he meant it as an encouragement.)

Expectations of unity: Nowhere in my employee handbook does it say we are a company free of conflict, where everyone gets along and peace reigns. Yet I seem to think that every meeting should produce only mutual respect and common vision, and maybe even some tangible result of teamwork (like a tree house, maybe, or a quilt). Imagine my disappointment when the only outcome of a meeting is another meeting, scheduled specifically when certain people can't attend (because they're not team players, you know). My expectations of consistent alignment—generally around my plans—are seldom met. God made us all different. Why am I taken aback when we act differently?

Expectations of fairness: My expectation that everyone (particularly me) will be treated equally and fairly crashes into reality quite a bit. One of my favorite lines from the movie *The Lion King* occurs when the mean lion Scar says, in that Jeremy Irons accent of his, "Life's not fair." I loved saying it to my kids as they encountered the bumps and bruises of life. I was helping toughen them up, I thought. So I was quite displeased when my son first said it to me in response to my whining about some petty issue at work. Kids today are so insolent.

I take some solace knowing that this expectation of fairness dates all the way back to Eve. Her sense of inequity that God had disqualified one tree as a source of sustenance was one of her motivations for taking the forbidden fruit. What a comfort to know that if there had been no Adam or Eve, I would still commit original sin!

Scriptural Expectations

Given the amount of Scripture that addresses misaligned expectations, I shouldn't be surprised by any of this. Paul and the writers of the Gospels—and even Jesus himself—urged us to have clear-sighted expectations. I go back to that foundational Scripture in John when Jesus tells the disciples about the difficult path ahead as a way to set their expectations. "I have told you these things, so that in me you may have peace. In this world you will have trouble. But take heart! I have overcome the world" (John 16:33).

Paul doesn't pull any punches when he tells the church at Thessalonica that they should have expected the afflictions they were experiencing. "For indeed when we were with you, we kept telling you in advance that we were going to suffer affliction; and so it came to pass, as you know" (I Thessalonians 3:4, NASB).

Peter also details the challenge of being a follower of Christ in a way that's hard to miss or misinterpret. "Dear friends, do not be surprised at the fiery ordeal that has come on you to test you, as though something strange were happening to you. But rejoice inasmuch as you participate in the sufferings of Christ, so that you may be overjoyed when his glory is revealed. If you are insulted because of the name of Christ, you are blessed, for the Spirit of glory and of God rests on you" (1 Peter 4:12–14).

Recalibrating My Expectations

Knowing all of this, what's my response? First, I need to recalibrate my expectations, realizing that bad things happen to good people, even when those good people are me. It's certainly more pleasant to always expect good outcomes, especially when, in the long run, there will be good outcomes. But I need to remind myself in the short-term that these things happen, they have happened to others, and I need to bounce back and reset as quickly as possible.

Of course, the challenge is not to go too far in the other direction, adopting the attitude that things will never work out. Always assuming the worst has the potential to build up anger, bitterness, resentment, and grouchiness, which is a handy recipe for alienating coworkers. (I know what you're thinking. Yes, it's too late for me. Save yourself!)

Second, I try to be content with what I have and where I am. This can come in the form of counting my blessings or gaining perspective by periodically stepping back from the daily work stresses. Again, Paul counsels us on the benefit of contentment when he writes, "But godliness with contentment is great gain. For we brought nothing into the world, and we can take nothing out of it. But if we have food and clothing, we will be content with that" (1 Timothy 6:6–8, NASB). When my expectations are calibrated along those lines, everything that happens beyond that is gravy!

Finally, the key to resiliently responding when life doesn't meet our expectations is to look beyond our short-term circumstances and rejoice in the permanence of a relationship with God. When we think about the relationship God invites us into compared to the frustration of daily life, we should be able to jump up and celebrate. And my celebration shouldn't be contingent on whether or not my expectations were met.

I don't always quote verses from the Old Testament book of Habakkuk, but this one bears repeating. "Even though the fig trees have no blossoms, and there are no grapes on the vines; even though the olive crop fails . . . yet I will rejoice in the Lord! I will be joyful in the God of my salvation" (Habakkuk 3:17–18, NLT).

It's a clear reminder that there is one expectation that we can hold on to: God has rescued us for something better, something that will exceed our expectations.

It's an encouraging thought. It's just not something I expected from Habakkuk.

Section 4:
MAKING FAITH REAL AT WORK

It's easy to say you are a Christian at work. But what is the
minimum level of action you need to take to really show it?
You may be surprised that the minimum acceptable level
is about twice as much as you're doing right now. These
chapters can help you get 5 percent closer while you sleep!

CHAPTER 17:

When Fear and Worry
Assume Control

One could say I am a fearful individual. I stew, I fret, I exude unease. My primary forms of exercise are jumping to conclusions and carrying things too far.

I worry. I worry a lot. I have always been a worrier. As a child, I worried that the tree next to our house would one day fall over and obliterate our home, scattering my stamp collection to the wind (my worries can be pretty specific). Today, I worry about my family, my stuff, my community, and my nation. I worry that termites are eating up my house foundation, that my knees are one brisk walk from giving out, that the world will someday run out of chocolate chip cookies. Left unchecked, my worry could easily make me curl into a ball in the corner, never to leave my house.

141

OK, OK, of course, I am once again exaggerating. Actually, there are only two things I worry about: things I can control and things I can't control.

The things I can control are a relatively small universe. I worry about whether I will leave on time for work. I worry about whether I am saving enough for retirement. I worry about whether my leisure suits are still in style.

But the funny thing is that I treat the second category—things I can't control—exactly like the first. I am smart enough to know I can't control them. But they could impact me, so I worry about them. It is a condition I believe the medical community calls "being irrational."

Worry at Work

Fear and worry cover all aspects of my life like a layer of dust at a dust manufacturing facility. But they are especially pernicious at work. (I don't know why I use words like *pernicious* when a much more common word, such as *harmful*, would work just fine. Maybe I figured you would think less of me if I wrote like a normal person. Or you would think I'm not very smart unless I use words like *pernicious* and *obliterate*. I worry about these things.)

The world of work is fertile ground for worry. Work incents us to focus on meeting the demands of the workplace, so it is not surprising that we put our faith in our work rather than our God. Because work is the means to pay for food and housing for my family, I spend a great deal of time worrying about it. I don't want anything bad to happen to my work because it could affect my income, my career path, and my very identity.

I know where you're going. You're thinking I've made work an idol. Well, of course, that's clearly not the case. It's just that my job is important to me. I constantly focus on it because it's the source of my security, my self-image, and it's the one thing capable of meeting all my needs.

(*Hmm* . . . perhaps I *have* made work an idol. I should worry about *that* more.)

Acting Out of Fear

Worry and fear are bad enough, in that they shift our focus away from what's truly important. But they also make people do strange things. Fear causes me to get angry when things don't go my way because I'm afraid of harming my career. Fear causes me to be disobedient because I don't see how waiting for events to occur or letting others have their way could possibly work out for me. Fear causes me to be discouraged because I start dwelling on bad outcomes. I fear not being in control or I fear that others may think I am less important or less powerful than they are. Rather than freely admitting I am human with the natural inclination to make mistakes, my fear causes me to lash out at others or blame someone else to shift the focus away from my shortcomings.

We get a great illustration of this dynamic in the Old Testament stories of Saul. The story of Saul's preparation to fight the Philistines in 1 Samuel 13 is a classic example of how fear causes someone to act badly. Saul had assembled his fighting men, and they were "quaking with fear." Some men were deserting, and Saul was getting anxious. Samuel was supposed to make an offering to ask God's blessing before battle, but he was late, so Saul made the offering himself.

So he said, "Bring me the burnt offering and the fellowship offerings." And Saul offered up the burnt offering. Just as he finished making the offering, Samuel arrived, and Saul went out to greet him.

"What have you done?" asked Samuel.

Saul replied, "When I saw that the men were scattering, and that you did not come at the set time, and that the Philistines were assembling at Mikmash, I thought, 'Now the Philistines will come down against me at Gilgal, and I have not sought the LORD's favor.' So I felt compelled to offer the burnt offering."

"You have done a foolish thing," Samuel said. "You have not kept the command the LORD your God gave you; if you had, he would have established your kingdom over Israel for all time. But now your kingdom will not endure; the LORD has sought out a man after his own heart and appointed him ruler of his people, because you have not kept the LORD's command." *(1 Samuel 13:10–14)*

Saul's fear that God wouldn't provide—at least according to Saul's timing—caused Saul to act on his own, and he lost God's favor in the process.

Author Os Hillman points[5] to another episode where fear got the better of Saul a few chapters later. After the warriors return from battle, the towns of Israel celebrated David's tens of thousands of enemies slain compared to the thousands of enemies Saul killed.

Saul was very angry; this refrain displeased him greatly. "They have credited David with tens of thousands," he thought, "but me with only thousands. What more can he get but the kingdom?" And from that time on Saul kept a close eye on David. (1 Samuel 18:8–9)

Saul's insecurity led him to try to control the situation, which created anger because the situation couldn't be controlled. It's a devastating illustration of the power of fear to derail a life and obstruct God's provision.

Finding Faith

Fortunately, worrying is not our only option. One of the great blessings of becoming a Christian was the good news that I didn't need to worry anymore. The joy of accepting Christ as my Savior meant I had a clear destination. That knowledge should override my worries and fears about the day-to-day issues. I just need to have faith. Faith is the inoculation and antidote for worry.

But becoming a Christian didn't mean that worry mysteriously left me, mostly because my daily concerns didn't mysteriously leave me. In fact, now I had a new concern. When I continued to get caught up in my earthly problems and kept running my worrying at full throttle, I now felt guilt. My worry clearly indicated that I didn't have faith, so what hope was there for me? It was disheartening and discouraging.

Over time, I've recognized that worry is a common trait, even among lifelong Christians. It is such a pernicious challenge (since I looked up the definition of *pernicious*, I thought I should get maximum use out of it) that Jesus made it a theme in his Sermon on the Mount. It was a top-of-mind concern for his listeners, so he spoke to their needs.

"Therefore I tell you, do not worry about your life, what you will eat or drink; or about your body, what you will wear. Is not life more than food, and the body more than clothes? Look at the birds of the air; they do not sow or reap or store away in barns, and yet your heavenly Father feeds them. Are you not much more valuable than they? Can any one of you by worrying add a single hour to your life?

"And why do you worry about clothes? See how the flowers of the field grow. They do not labor or spin. Yet I tell you that not even Solomon in all his splendor was dressed like one of these. If that is how God clothes the grass of the field, which is here today and tomorrow is thrown into the fire, will he not much more clothe you— you of little faith? So do not worry, saying, 'What shall we eat?' or 'What shall we drink?' or 'What shall we wear?' For the pagans run after all these things, and your heavenly Father knows that you need them. But seek first his kingdom and his righteousness, and all these things will be given to you as well. Therefore do not worry about tomorrow, for tomorrow will worry about itself. Each day has enough trouble of its own." (Matthew 6:25-34)

That message reassures me. Yes, I should live that way. And I continually work to live like that. But for Jesus to devote so much attention to the topic, I take solace knowing it's a common issue and I'm not the first person to struggle with it. And I note his aside—"you of little faith"—as reinforcement that faith is the key to stopping the worry train.

Start with Faith in God

The real question is what we have faith *in*. It's not a safe bet to have faith that everything will work out in my favor. We're not promised that work will be smooth, coworkers will be kind, or our salaries will be more than we can spend. (In fact, sometimes those things don't happen for the very purpose of *making* us more faithful.) But God does promise that he is in control, he is with us, he will strengthen and guide us, and we will have an abundant and eternal life.

God can be trusted for this because it is repeated throughout Scripture. The Psalms alone describe God's faithfulness in dozens of verses. It's God's nature to be faithful.

- For the word of the Lord is right and true; he is faithful in all he does. (Psalm 33:4)
- For great is your love, reaching to the heavens; your faithfulness reaches to the skies. (Psalm 57:10)
- For the Lord is good and his love endures forever; his faithfulness continues through all generations. (Psalm 100:5)
- Not to us, Lord, not to us but to your name be the glory, because of your love and faithfulness. (Psalm 115:1)
- The Lord is righteous in all his ways and faithful in all he does. (Psalm 145:17)

For a further dose of faith, meditate on Psalm 136, where every line concludes with the refrain, "His faithful love endures forever"—twenty-six times, by my count.

But I also know God is faithful because I have seen it in my own life. It is humbling to reflect on the many times when I have stressed, pleaded, and prayed to God for an outcome. Sometimes he delivered what I requested, sometimes he delivered something better, and sometimes, despite my heartbreak, he didn't deliver what I wanted. But even in those cases, I felt comfort and eventually recognized that things turned out anyway. That's been a wonderful benefit of writing out my prayers as part of my morning Bible study. It's incredibly encouraging to be able to look back on those times when I was scared and worried and remember how I asked God to intercede. With the passage of time, being able to review those prayers and see how God answered them has been extraordinarily encouraging. Of course, God didn't answer every prayer as I wanted—or as I specifically prayed. But to see how things worked out over time, again and again, helps me move from away from worrying toward trusting God more every day.

The Illusion of Control

For me, here's the most convincing argument that worry is silly and faith is smart: I have so little control over the outcomes I desire. I have convinced myself—and my annual pay raise depends on other people believing—that I can make things happen. But when you think about it, I'm pretty incapable. I can't make the sun come up; I can't control what other people think; I can't even control the passage of time. That's all God, all the time.

I love how Mark Roberts describes it in one of his devotions for *The High Calling*:

In truth, you and I depend on God each moment, even if we don't recognize it. The very fabric of creation relies on God's power. You and I need him for our next breath, our next thought, our next action. The more we acknowledge our dependence on the Lord, the more we will learn to rely on his faithful provision, and the less we will worry, because God is faithful.[6]

When I think about it like that, I am inspired to put my worry aside. I haven't swung to complete success. But growing in my faith by consciously looking at how God keeps his promises is a wise choice.

Worry is fruitless and pointless.

But that doesn't mean it's not pernicious.

CHAPTER 18:

Mercy and/or Grace and/or Both

M ercy and grace are pretty amazing elements of the Christian faith. But given their interrelated nature, I often confuse the two. Our pastor characterized mercy as not experiencing the bad consequences that our actions deserve. He defined grace as getting something better than we deserve. I tend to blur them because they both result in getting a better outcome than I would otherwise get if grace and/or mercy weren't part of the equation.

Between the two, you have something like spiritual Bubble Wrap—not guaranteeing you won't be jostled in life but certainly helping make the journey a lot safer.

I'm a big fan of these elements of our faith, but they are not something I'm good at incorporating into my work life. Oh, I receive them—in abundance. If I didn't, what we think of as Tom probably wouldn't be much more than an oily spot on the floor. But I tend to fall down on giving grace and mercy to others. I'm figuratively like a huge jelly-filled donut, oozing and overflowing with the mercy and grace I have received. Yet I don't share my jelly . . . er, mercy and grace . . . with others.

That's an issue.

Tangible Mercy

I have been the beneficiary of mercy and/or grace at least a gazillion times over the years. They come in the form of forgiveness, kindness, generosity, and leniency. Yes, I have had my share of stumbles and career setbacks, but not in the frequency and severity that one would expect given my ill-informed and poorly performed activities. Each time, I was saved by the kind responses of others.

- I experienced grace recently from the coworker who spent hours walking me through a technical concept so I could capture it for a presentation for the board of directors, even though the coworker was giving up his time and had to work after hours to complete his day job. His efforts saved me from sending the board members a presentation that looked like it had been written by a middle schooler.

- Mercy was evident from the executive who focused our team on doing an after-oops assessment to ensure a problem didn't happen again versus lining us all up for a figurative firing squad (and potential literal firing).

- The colleague who caught my error in a document before it was distributed throughout the company gave me a similarly generous gift, especially since she didn't need to spend her time doing what wasn't her job.

Those were just the most recent examples in a long line of mercy and grace episodes. In each case, I benefitted from a better outcome than my own efforts would warrant.

But when it comes time for me to give these same gifts to others, I drop the ball. It happened again recently when a colleague was tasked with providing information for an executive presentation for a trade association meeting. The deadline was approaching, and we hadn't received her material. I was getting stressed. Rather than calmly seek her out to determine the status of the request, I publicly unloaded on her, accusing her of threatening the success of this project, and maybe the company's very existence.

But she responded with a graciousness superior to my actions. She calmly explained that she had met the deadline, but she had provided the information directly to the executive who needed it.

It was another opportunity to think maybe I should try to do better in this area.

Being Lousy at Mercy and Grace

I may be bad at extending grace and mercy to my coworkers, but at least I'm good at rationalizing why I'm bad at it. The basic problem is that this generosity is not in my (human) nature. Maybe it's hard for me because I live and work in a fallen world, or I'm the result of generations of teaching and reinforcing self-sufficiency. But granting forgiveness seems like a foreign concept. I'm pretty darn selfish. I think fear plays a part, too. I'm afraid that someone else's failure will reflect badly on me. Rather than all go down as a team, I want to make sure blame is securely placed on "not me." Forgiving someone could almost seem as though I'm somehow culpable for this failure. It all adds up to a real reluctance to forgive and forget—especially in the competitive, driven world of work.

Even on those rare occasions when I express some sentiment of grace, it's pretty pathetic. It's much less than a God-sized portion. It's more of a micro memory card portion, if that micro memory card didn't have very much memory.

Crying Over Spilled Milk

My daughter is still traumatized from an episode when she was a preschooler and we went to the grocery store to buy a gallon of milk. After we checked out, she insisted on carrying it, even though it weighed more than she did. She was happily trying to swing it back and forth on this fun adventure with her loving daddy when she lost her grip. The plastic jug fell from her hands and landed with a splat in the parking lot, pouring out my precious milk. I was furious, and I let her know. The poor little adorable thing burst into tears, but I was unmoved. I sent that four-year-old back into the grocery store to buy another gallon of milk with her own money while I sat in the car and waited.

I didn't do that.

In fact, *not* taking that extreme step was a sign of my merciful munificence. Instead, all I did was lecture her all the way home about personal responsibility, financial encumbrance, and gravity, and I made her eat dry cereal at breakfast the next day. I thought I was showing mercy. Think how much worse it would have been if she had to use three years of her allowance to buy a replacement gallon of milk! (I also wasn't very gracious when it came to allowance amounts.) Years later, the fact that she remembers that story vividly and painfully and still tears up whenever she tells it, tells me that maybe she didn't see the whole episode as a monument of mercy.

An Important Part of Our Faith

Showing mercy and grace at work is important because fostering better outcomes than people expect is an area where we Christians can truly distinguish ourselves in the workplace. Offering "compassionate or kindly forbearance" or "unmerited acts of kindness, compassion, or favor" can demonstrate that people of faith have a broader perspective than those whose focus is only the rewards of work. For a hurting world, demonstrating such kindness and compassion to others can be a great way to reflect the benefits of faith.

It's also important to share this graciousness at work because the Bible writers spent so much time talking about mercy and grace. Mercy tends to get top billing, probably because the great gift of eternal life in spite of our sinful ways is maximum mercy. But grace is a dominant theme in Paul's writings, too. Mercy and grace appear in some of the best-known illustrations and parables in Scripture.

- Many individuals, including a man whose son is demon-possessed (see Matthew 17), two blind men (see Matthew 20), and Bartimaeus (see Mark 10), all call out to Jesus for mercy when he is near.
- The cry for mercy is a big difference in the prayers of the hypocritical Pharisee and the tax collector. "The Pharisee stood by himself and prayed: 'God, I thank you that I am not like other people—robbers, evildoers, adulterers—or even like this tax collector. I fast twice a week and give a tenth of all I get.' But the tax collector stood at a distance. He would not even look up to heaven, but beat his

breast and said, 'God, have mercy on me, a sinner'" (Luke 18:10–13).

- Mercy is the answer to the question Jesus asked after sharing the story of the Good Samaritan. "'Which of these three do you think was a neighbor to the man who fell into the hands of robbers?' The expert in the law replied, 'The one who had mercy on him.' Jesus told him, 'Go and do likewise'" (Luke 10:36–37).
- Paul describes the redeeming value of grace in saving us from sin. "For sin shall no longer be your master, because you are not under the law, but under grace" (Romans 6:14).
- And Paul points to God's grace as providing the power and strength beyond the burden he carried. "But he said to me, 'My grace is sufficient for you, for my power is made perfect in weakness.' Therefore I will boast all the more gladly about my weaknesses, so that Christ's power may rest on me" (2 Corinthians 12:9).

God is a God of mercy and grace, as evidenced by his continual withholding of destruction on the Israelites throughout the Old Testament. (And closer to home, evidenced by my own redemption so I don't have to spend an eternity away from him.) Given how important these concepts are in our faith, it's safe to say they should also be an important part of our work.

Working to Do Better

It's pretty clear I need to work on this. Once again, it needs to be less about my effort and more about my submission. The ability to bestow graciousness on another person is truly a supernatural, spiritual thing. Any generosity I do give comes from somewhere beyond me. It has to be spirit-inspired because, well, Tom-inspired is just not inspirational.

But I can still act. I can do things that reflect mercy and grace. I can rise above the stress of the moment and focus on the other person's needs. I can forgive someone when I think I've been treated unfairly. I can choose to bite my tongue, even when someone is doing something that is just foolish and pointless and . . . (I'm still working on this.)

Showing grace and mercy means being intentional about seeing people through God's eyes. Scripture makes it clear that God spends less time looking at the situation and instead focuses on the heart, so that should be my model, too. Rather than react to the moment, I should respond with a gentleness built on an eternal perspective.

I think one of the most moving Scriptures showing Jesus's compassion comes in Matthew's Gospel as Jesus is looking at the crowds before him. "When he saw the crowds, he had compassion on them, because they were harassed and helpless, like sheep without a shepherd" (Matthew 9:36). I picture Jesus, with a heavy heart, wanting so much for people to flourish through his better way. It's no surprise that his next line is encouragement for the disciples to pray for workers because the harvest is so plentiful.

If I had to guess, I'd say he was talking about me being that worker who shows compassion to others.

If nothing else (and here's where I get back to making it all about me), I should show such generosity to others because it makes me feel good. I've been taken aback by the sincere appreciation people have expressed to me when I act in mercy (my daughter being the notable exception). Being merciful and graceful—being kind, offering forgiveness, giving someone a second chance—can feel wonderful. When all else fails, appealing to my selfish self-interest is a good motivator for me to do the right thing.

Mercy Bucket

Because here's the thing: I don't have to be stingy with mercy or grace. They are not going to run out. My overflowing jelly donut has jelly to spare. As a result of coming under the saving grace of Jesus Christ, I get to enjoy mercy and grace continually flowing over me whether I share them or not. Quoting Paul again, God's grace is sufficient, which means I don't need anything more. And Jesus gives us a clear-cut example of how to share this grace and mercy with others.

It's a lesson I learned with the spilled milk experience with my daughter. Oh, my response was miserable. But the fact that she is willing to still acknowledge me in public and sometimes is willing to spend time with me is quite humbling.

That feels like mercy.

Or maybe it's grace.

Or maybe it's both. I get confused.

CHAPTER 19

The Obstacle of Obedience

You wouldn't think that obedience would be a problem for me. As a child, I was very compliant. When my mother told me to do my chores, I did them promptly. I took out the trash, cleaned my room, and ate my vegetables (albeit sometimes with gagging noises when there were brussels sprouts staring me down). I complied with obedience.

But something happened when I grew up. Suddenly, I saw obedience as a horrible, unfair burden that got in the way of my desires. It called me to set aside my intentions, and it ruined my plans. I responded to calls for obedience by reverting to a toddler stage, insisting that, "I can do it myself!"

Yes, the truth is that I'm bad at obedience. I don't consistently follow the faith instructions we've all been given. That's unfortunate because obedience is a necessary part of living out our faith excellently.

Obedient to What?

As Christians, we've received a marvelous collection of wisdom that benefits us if we would only follow it. The Bible is chock full of rules, guidelines, and admonitions, so you have lots of principles from which to choose. You could seek to live according to the Ten Commandments, Proverbs, or the letters of Paul. Or all of the above. (If you choose to live your life according to the Old Testament codes of Leviticus, please contact me. I'm just curious to see what that looks like in practice.)

I'm drawn to Jesus's life principles outlined in the Sermon on the Mount (see Matthew 5–7). Within these 111 verses are clear instructions about how we should live, steward our finances, interact with and serve others, and even deal with our emotions. You can throw a lawn dart at these pages (but please, only use the super-safe foam darts with the squishy tips) and you'll hit a line of Scripture that offers life-giving wisdom.

Those are the verses I consistently don't obey.

For example, I generally disregard Matthew 5:42: "Give to the one who asks you, and do not turn away from the one who wants to borrow from you." I'm terrible at this. I have an inflated sense of ownership of my stuff, even if it's not really my stuff. I was on a business trip with a colleague once, and he asked if he could borrow my car so he could go meet a friend for dinner. I hemmed and hawed and made excuses why he couldn't, even though I had no plans for the car that night. And the kicker was that it wasn't even my car. It was a rental car! Yet I expressed all kinds of reasons why he shouldn't take it. (What if his spleen burst while he was driving, and I was without a car to drive to the airport to meet the emergency helicopter to retrieve the replacement spleen airlifted to him? Huh!? Who'd be sorry then!?) By the end of our conversation, he was prying the keys out of my tightly clutched fingers. I wouldn't be surprised if he made up the whole dinner-with-a-friend thing just to have some time away from his jerk of a coworker.

Or this: "But when you give to someone in need, don't let your left hand know what your right hand is doing. Give your gifts in private, and your Father, who sees everything, will reward you" (Matthew 6:3–4, NLT). I don't even try at this one, especially at work. If I give someone the gift of my time, or wise counsel, or business insight . . . well, I want people to know. I offered a colleague my thoughts on a presentation he was giving to a group of customers. On the surface, this looked admirable. I was helping him succeed! But when the presentation was a success, I made sure to let everyone from the mailroom to the executive suite know what a (now inflated) contribution I had made to the presentation. No one seemed interested, and the nighttime cleaning staff was almost rude trying to leave the building as I told the story of my amazing assistance.

Or there's Matthew 6:19-20: "Do not store up for yourselves treasures on earth, where moths and vermin destroy, and where thieves break in and steal. But store up for yourselves treasures in heaven." I can't give you a thorough accounting of my treasures stored in heaven, but you can bet your homeowners insurance policy that I can provide an exhaustive list of all the stuff I have on earth, from my priceless college t-shirt collection all the way to my favorite coffee mug. (It's the one that says, "World's Okay-est Employee.")

A former pastor interpreted this passage to mean that what we store in heaven is the people and relationships we will take with us to our eternal life. But I am disobedient in collecting a big heavenly treasure trove, too, since I also disobey Matthew 7:1: "Do not judge, or you too will be judged."

I could go on (remember, there are 111 verses in these three chapters), but you get the point. Although Jesus is clear and vivid in describing the right way to live, I choose to disobey.

Cornerstone of Faith

My disobedience is not good for me (or the people around me). Obedience is a tangible act of faith. Obedience is the key to receiving God's blessings. Scripture shows how highly God values obedience. From the beginning, God gave Adam and Eve instructions and expected compliance. When God was ramping up the nation of Israel, he provided a lot of directions that included the concept of obedience. He told the people, "Love the LORD your God and keep his requirements, his decrees, his laws and his commands always" (Deuteronomy 11:1).

Jesus simply and clearly communicates spiritual truth when he tells us that obedience is core to following him. "If you love me, obey my commandments" (John 14:15, NLT). Obedience is inseparable from our Christian faith.

A former pastor was vigilant about teaching our congregation about the necessity of obedience. Presumably appropriately, it felt as though his messages were directed at me. (He's the one who told me that I know more Scripture than I am obedient to. He thought he was being helpful, or funny; I'm not sure which.) He used a memorable illustration that we are all vessels and need to decide what fills us. If we're being obedient, we are filled with Jesus, available to pour out to others. If we fill our vessels with ourselves, then all we have to pour out to others is our broken, selfish selves. (The way he told it made it seem even worse.)

Working Against It

As I demonstrate every day, obedience to God's Word can get problematic because it runs headfirst into human free will. In my case, that free will sometimes can be surprisingly strong, as well as whiny and petulant. When I'm afraid I won't get my way, I have been known to deflect, rationalize, justify, claim superior insight, make excuses, call for waivers and exemptions, and blame others rather than joyfully submitting my will. Rather than just obeying, I exert a lot of energy finding ways not to.

Of course, my approach is not only wrong but also downright dangerous. God repeatedly reminds us in Scripture that there are consequences when we don't obey. Several faith leaders experienced some disastrous outcomes when they didn't obey. Moses didn't get to enter the Promised Land because he let his frustration with the people cause him to act outside of God's call (see Numbers 20). David earned a plague for his people when he decided to count his troops, indicating that he felt his strength came in numbers, not in God (see 2 Samuel 24). Jonah spent time cleaning off fish guts after he refused God's directive to go to Nineveh (see Jonah 1). And Peter suffered what I surmise was an excruciating ordeal when he realized that he had denied Jesus three times, just as Jesus had predicted. To make matters worse, all four Gospel authors showcase Peter's failure (see Matthew 26, Mark 14, Luke 22, and John 18).

If faith leaders experience these kinds of setbacks and suffering when they are disobedient, I should anticipate that the same difficulties will find me.

Move from Thinking to Acting

Intellectually, I understand the concept of obedience. It's hard to miss the vital role it plays in expressing our love for God and aligning ourselves with God's plans for us. I know that obedience is important. But knowing is not good enough. I also need to act on my knowing.

It's noteworthy how Jesus concludes the 111 verses in the Sermon on the Mount. After outlining how we should live, he reinforces the critical need to make these things real by sharing the parable of the man building his house.

> "Therefore everyone who hears these words of mine and puts them into practice is like a wise man who built his house on the rock. The rain came down, the streams rose, and the winds blew and beat against that house; yet it did not fall, because it had its foundation on the rock. But everyone who hears these words of mine and does not put them into practice is like a foolish man who built his house on sand. The rain came down, the streams rose, and the winds blew and beat against that house, and it fell with a great crash." *(Matthew 7:24–27)*

The Need to Surrender

Obedience begins with the simple act of surrendering. Again, it's a super simple concept. It means to cease resistance and submit to authority. Easy, right? In fact, it should be freeing. Instead of feeling the burden of making decisions and working hard to push outcomes, all I need to do is stop resisting and let God lead.

But it's really hard in practice. Over the years, I've been taught, either intentionally or unintentionally, that *surrender* is another word for "quit," which rhymes with "loser." The concept of surrender, even surrendering to God, feels like a sign of weakness. What's worse, sometimes *surrender* looks a lot like "wait" or "pause" or even "stop." That's especially troubling to me, because "stop" may mean scrapping my plans or ceasing my striving. But my life and especially my career have reinforced that striving and effort is good and passivity is bad. I tend to think that if I try harder, I can finally push the rock up the hill, instead of allowing God to move the rock where he wants it. Or, in a real paradigm shift, maybe God wants to leave the rock where it is and move me instead. (Mind blown.)

Surrendering may mean that we need to release things we've been clinging to, from our finances to our identities built upon our work. Obedience to God can scrape away the elements of pride, selfishness, and self-sufficiency. For most of us, that's hard work along the path to spiritual growth. But the destination is alignment with God and spiritual maturity for us.

Start with God's Plan

True obedience is not about taking my path, but rather taking the path God has chosen for me and continually seeking his guidance for course corrections along the way. That happens in prayer. It's knowing that God's will for our obedience requires listening for his direction, reading Scripture for guidance, and engaging with Christian friends who have the discernment to share what they hear. I can't start with my plans and then see if God lines up. I need to reverse that order. Sometimes the plan I want is also the plan God has for me, but I can't jump ahead.

Finally, if we're not clear what obedience looks like, we have a perfect example in the actions of Jesus. His process of obedience followed that same path: stopping, surrendering, and praying. And he did it in a way that helps us learn from his example.

One of the most startling lines of Scripture for me is Hebrews 5:8: "Although He was a Son, He learned obedience from the things which He suffered" (NASB). That was shocking to me.

Even Jesus, who lived a life of obedience all the way to the cross, learned obedience through the trials he experienced. His prayers in the Garden of Gethsemane show us clearly what that obedience looks like. "'Abba, Father,' he cried out, 'everything is possible for you. Please take this cup of suffering away from me. Yet I want your will to be done, not mine'" (Mark 14:36). He laid down his will to accept the plan of God.

It's a challenging reminder that obedience doesn't mean I will get my way. Consequently, I have to keep the spiritual rewards of obedience—the blessings of God—front and center. I also must be obedient in waiting for them, because they may not happen in the timetable I desire or expect.

Second Chances to Obedience

It is also crucially important to recognize that obedience, like other aspects of my faith, isn't something I have to do in my own effort. I love the quote attributed to former United Press International religion writer Louis Cassels that God gives us the strength to be obedient if we ask for it.

> Obey . . . take up your cross . . . deny yourself. . . . It all sounds very hard. It is hard. Anyone who tells you differently is peddling spiritual soothing syrup, not real Christianity. And yet, in a strangely paradoxical way, it is also easy. With every cross that we lift in obedience to Christ comes the strength to carry it. It is always a package deal.

I need to lean on God's grace to help me truly embrace obedience. And I believe God is patient with us on our journey to mastering this. I look again to Jonah for another aspect of the process of obedience. Even after he was disobedient to God's call to minister to the people of Nineveh and suffered the consequences of his disobedience, God called him to obedience *again*.

> Now the word of the LORD came to Jonah the second time, saying, "Arise, go to Nineveh, the great city, and proclaim to it the proclamation which I am going to tell you." So Jonah got up and went to Nineveh according to the word of the Lord. *(Jonah 3:1–3, NASB)*

If the God of second chances once again calls Jonah to be obedient, I can take courage that I should keep working at this. Perhaps I will do better the second time around.

Granted, I could be obedient the first time and save myself the fishing experience, but let's not get ahead of ourselves . . .

CHAPTER 20:

Shining the Light for Others

L et's pretend you have received the greatest gift in the whole world. It's better than socks, or your own island, or a factory that produces endless chocolate chip cookies. It's a pretty awesome gift. But suppose after you get this gift, you decide not to share it with anyone else. You decide it is such a good gift that you don't want anyone else to have something as nice as you have.

But this isn't a typical gift like socks. It's a gift that grows each time it is passed on. The more you share it, the more you have to give. You can give it to people over and over and over. Every stranger you meet, every family member you love, every family member you don't love—they all can receive this gift. And when they do, the gift just becomes more precious and valuable for you.

After all that, if you still hesitate or even decline to give this gift away, what does that make you? Maybe a Class A Jerk? Maybe a selfish, self-absorbed mumpsimus? (Which is not only a real word apparently, but also an apt description of how you would be acting.)

If you did that, you should at the very least feel guilty and, at most, excluded from civil society.

Welcome to my guilty world.

Sharing the Good News

The gift I'm talking about, of course, is what we often call the "Good News." It's the amazing story of God's compassion and love for each of us that resulted in sending his Son Jesus, first as a bridge to God and then, in Jesus's death, as the substitute for our sins. In return, we get an eternity in the presence of our Creator. Pretty darn good gift! But once I accepted that amazing gift, I have been embarrassingly reluctant to spread it around.

The reasons, to paraphrase the demon-possessed man, are legion. For starters, maybe the most superficial excuse is that I don't always stop to think that other people haven't been in a position to receive this gift before now. For some of us, our friends and family are centered around attending church, and we may not recognize that many of our coworkers haven't had the same experiences we've had. We may be the only Christians our coworkers ever get to know well.

I'm also reluctant to share my faith because, frankly, engaging with people is a messy thing. Oh, superficially, I am good with people. Great, even. When I superficially interact with people at the office, we semi-smile at one another in the hallway, perhaps mumbling something heartfelt like, "Morning," and then go on without feeling any need for further interaction. I've been known to nod at other people. I sometimes hold doors open for them. I may even gently tell a person when he or she has dropped a glove. Beyond that, however, I find that people take an *incredible* amount of energy and time. Engaging with people invariably means I will have to go back to my desk and work at a more hurried pace, or work longer, because I've wasted so much valuable time engaging with them. It's a real inconvenience.

I wish I could tell you that I was kidding. But those thoughts have gone through my head. And that's after I knew better. Knowledge is one thing; acting on it is something different.

Another excuse for not sharing my faith is that my insecurities get in the way. I'm worried the other person may be put off by the ham-handed way I tell my story. If I share my faith poorly, I worry I may make it sound bad and have the effect of discouraging the other person from learning more. And I'm nervous they may be one of those people who think people take an *incredible* amount of energy and time. Trying to engage them will just make them hate people more—and me in particular.

I recognize that, as a practicing Christian, I'm supposed to be the example of Jesus. But that is a horrible amount of pressure, if you ask me. I know that God can work miracles through me if I am obedient. But if I'm expected to present a pure and holy presence in front of my coworkers eight, nine, or eighteen hours a day, I just think that's a lot to ask. I fall more in the Peter-the-night-Jesus-was-betrayed category here.

"Say, Tom, the guys in the lunchroom said you were a Christian. Is that right?

"Me, no, uh, I'm a Piston. You know, a Detroit Pistons fan. Go team!"

Of course, I'm exaggerating. I'm probably flattering myself if I thought I had provided enough evidence for the guys in the lunchroom to think I'm a Christian in the first place.

Threatening Evangelism

Part of my problem is that I keep thinking of sharing my faith as something I need to force on other people. I presume that since I have received this great gift, I need to press it into their hands before the elevator door closes, like some Cold War East German courier passing microfilm in a bad spy novel.

But that presumes this gift is something they don't want, like a brussels sprout casserole. If that had been Jesus's evangelism model, he would have gathered a band of hoodlums and hooligans (yes, I was raised in the 1920s) who went around being tough and intimidating to try to force people to follow them. The fact that Jesus took a more compassionate approach probably offers a lesson for me.

Start with Felt Needs

Time and time again, Jesus interacts with people in Scripture first with a conversation about their needs. It must have given him such a heavy heart to see how this fallen world had injured God's children. I'm always afraid I will be discouraged when I have similar deep interactions with others. But what I feel instead is a sense of compassion, undoubtedly not unlike Jesus's response. It was a turning point in my faith when I opened my heart to the people around me. Eventually sharing with coworkers my wife's cancer diagnosis taught me the value and benefit of being vulnerable. The warmth and care I received filled me with gratitude. When we are vulnerable with one another, we experience one another's hurts, pains, frustrations, and shared sadness. What results is a much deeper connection.

It comes down to this: *People need Jesus.* It's a simple phrase, but it captures a lot. I think it to myself when I come across someone who is struggling. And sometimes I say it when someone frustrates me so much that "People need Jesus" is about the kindest thing I can say! It reminds me that, even when we may not think so, we are incomplete without Jesus. Without him, people will keep searching for job recognition, salary increases, or worse to fill their lives. With him, they have a chance to experience a life that is so much more fulfilling.

So I need to share this gift I have received. But how do I do it well? Someone once advised me that we all need to have three things as a foundation before we share our hearts. I'm a big fan of preparation and lists, so I appreciated the guidance.

- Be prayerful
- Be ready
- Be real

Be prayerful. I am only moved out of my comfort zone to provide a positive a witness to my coworkers if I lead with my faith, not with myself. That means keeping my prayer life strong. I will too easily revert to my own lazy, passive state if I'm not seeking God's wisdom and insight through prayer and study. I also get in my own way when I try to do it myself. So I need to pray.

When I pray for my coworkers, a couple of things happen. One, I stop seeing them through my eyes and start seeing them through God's eyes. In my eyes, they are annoying and time-wasting. Through his perspective, they are beautiful, holy, and in need of life-giving relationships.

The second thing that happens when I pray for my coworkers is that I become sensitive to their needs. I stop seeing Jane as always being late in the morning and start seeing her as a single mom trying to juggle daycare drop-offs. I see Dwayne not as someone looking for a fight but as someone who's looking for a little respect. I see Dave as someone who spends way too much time talking about Dr. Who. (I still pray for him, but I'll be honest, I'm not optimistic here.) When I'm sensitive to others' needs, I can lift those needs up to God and ask what I should do to help.

Because I am prone to self-promotion ahead of God-promotion, I also must be prayed up to make sure I'm both appropriately motivated and properly positioned. If I'm not, my own insecurities, fears, and ego easily overtake me, mess with my intentions, and derail my effectiveness. Rather than caring for their needs, I can often try to serve others primarily to make myself feel better about myself. (What I meant to say is that I have seen examples of this in, uh, other people.)

Be ready. I always thought that evangelizing coworkers would happen on my timetable. I figured that when I was ready, God would put a person-in-need in my path, make me aware that he or she needed a good talking-to, and then one day I'd take that person to a nearby cathedral or national park for "the talk" (you know, to let the full awesome God atmosphere enhance the persuasiveness of my message).

Not surprisingly, it doesn't work that way. You never know when someone will ask you to explain why you have patience with your enemies, why you talk more about your family than your golf score, or why you think of others before you think of yourself. (I haven't had that last one happen yet, but with God all things are possible.) You need to be ready at all times to explain. You never know when that door will open.

It's described beautifully by Peter: "But in your hearts revere Christ as Lord. Always be prepared to give an answer to everyone who asks you to give the reason for the hope that you have. But do this with gentleness and respect" (1 Peter 3:15–16). We never know when the time will come, so don't be caught off guard.

A few years ago, I was on a photo shoot with a photographer and his assistant. I'd been driving them around in my car when the assistant noticed the fish symbol on the back of it. (I tell people I need to have a fish symbol on my car so they know I am a Christian—they can't tell by my driving.) He asked me (with a hint of incredulity, I thought later), "Are you a fisher of men?" Of course, I knew what he was talking about, but I didn't proudly express, "Why, yes, my good man, I am a follower of my Lord and Savior Jesus Christ, seeking to complete the Great Commission by spreading the Good News to all the world. How about you?" Instead, I mumbled something about how a friend of mine worked at a Christian bookstore, and I felt like I needed to buy something on her first day, and isn't the weather warm for this time of year?

I still have some work to do in this area.

Be real. When talking with others about faith, there's probably no better strategy than to *share your heart*. I find a lot of answers in the Bible, but there are still many things I can't explain. I don't know what heaven looks like, I can't explain grace, and I don't know why Job doesn't have better friends. I believe the unknowns and the mysteries are there for a reason. They exist to build and shape our faith.

Rather than focus on what I don't know, I can share what I do know, which is how Jesus has affected my life. I can describe how my perspective on thousands of things has changed and how my priorities have shifted since I accepted Christ. I can't argue theology with anyone, including my children (especially my children). But I can explain what's different inside of me and describe my continued dependence on God's grace to make it through each day. I happen to be an expert on that topic.

And that's what people care about anyway. Once they are ready to build their relationship with Jesus, the Bible is excellent for shedding light on the ways of God. Besides, I figure that's what pastors are for. But to get people's attention in the first place, they need to know what's in it for them. And hopefully, what's in it for them is a perspective that is secure, selfless, and heavenly oriented.

A Gang of Fishing People

If this is all starting to feel a bit heavy, we can rejoice knowing we don't have to do this all alone. Believing that I am the only one divinely chosen to share the Good News with my coworkers appeals to my ego. But that's not how it works. Even Jesus had others with him most of the time. My experiences may not be enticing to Jane, but Susan's experiences might be. And we also encourage one another when we know we are all trying to do better at sharing our faith. A wise person told me that generally people don't come to faith because of one person, but because of their contact with dozens of believers. I'm taking that to the bank. I don't have to explain the Transfiguration or the Resurrection. In that person's chain of contacts, I'm just supposed to be real about my faith experience.

Keeping It Simple

Evangelism can seem complicated. But I came across some verses recently that drove home the very best model for effectively sharing our faith. It was the story of Paul and Silas, beaten and imprisoned in Philippi, and how their response made an impression on the people around them.

> After they had been severely flogged, they were thrown into prison, and the jailer was commanded to guard them carefully. When he received these orders, he put them in the inner cell and fastened their feet in the stocks. About midnight Paul and Silas were praying and singing hymns to God, and the other prisoners were listening to them. Suddenly there was such a violent earthquake that the foundations of the prison were shaken. At once all the prison doors flew open, and everyone's chains came loose. The jailer woke up, and when he saw the prison doors open, he drew his sword and was about to kill himself because he thought the prisoners had escaped. But Paul shouted, "Don't harm yourself! We are all here!"
> The jailer called for lights, rushed in, and fell trembling before Paul and Silas. He then brought them out and asked, "Sirs, what must I do to be saved?"
> They replied, "Believe in the Lord Jesus, and you will be saved—you and your household." Then they spoke the word of the Lord to him and to all the others in his house. At that hour of the night the jailer took them and washed their wounds; then immediately he and all his household were baptized. The jailer brought them into his house and set a meal before them; he was filled with joy because he had come to believe in God—he and his whole household. (*Acts 16:23–34*)

I am drawn to that story because God is at the center of it. Paul and Silas aren't threatening the jailer, telling him to believe or "It's curtains for you, big guy!" They are praising God when others would think they would be at their lowest point. It's powerful because it illustrates a simple principle that we can use in our evangelism: People always want something that is better than what they currently have. For the jailer, Paul and Silas represented something so superior that the jailer couldn't help but seek it for himself and his family. I may not be singing God's praises when I am in jail (and, let's face it, I probably would be complaining that the stocks are too tight or the walls are too damp). But what effect will it have on coworkers if they see me singing God's praises during my down days at work? If people see real, tangible results and a positive change in my life, why wouldn't they clamor to ask me how they can get that, too?

That still can feel like a lot of pressure. But it shouldn't. I have been given this amazing gift, better than socks, and I owe it to others to share it.

Would you like to know more?

I'm happy to tell you my story.

Let's step into the cathedral and/or national park.

CHAPTER 21:

Holy Travel to Tahiti

Whenever I travel for business these days, I keep my eyes tightly closed. I do that so I can imagine my travel as a glamorous and sophisticated throwback to an idealized past. In that world, uniformed flight attendants serve full-course airline meals on fine dishes with hot towels, even though I'm only flying from Duluth to Fargo. My destination hotel is a classic downtown accommodation, with coat-wearing bellboys waiting to take my bags and sharp-dressed staff behind the counter greeting me by name. They have my registration in hand, because I called and talked to the same concierge who has worked for this fine lodging establishment for forty-four years. The hotel dining room always has my steak dinner ready promptly at

6:00 p.m., and they know which dressing to put on my garnished house salad (bleu cheese, slightly chilled, and spelled correctly).

It's not easy to live in this travel fantasy, of course, because business travel today is very different. Travel of any duration can be a soul-crushing experience, leaving a traveler beaten down and broken. Loyalty programs aren't loyal. Neither are airlines; they lose baggage and passengers. The rental car company runs out of cars, the hotel has no record of my reservation, and the manager of the short-staffed restaurant apologizes that tonight, due to supply chain issues, they only have olives and guacamole on the menu.

So I travel with my eyes closed, relying on the kindness of strangers to help me find my airline seat (at least strangers who aren't similarly wandering around with their eyes closed). I try to drive on Interstate 94 through Chicago with one hand over my eyes (which still makes me a better driver than most everyone else on Chicago highways).

Bait and Switch

What does travel have to do with navigating faith at work? It's quite applicable. In full transparency, this is not really a chapter about travel. It's a chapter about personal holiness and how we act when we don't think anyone is looking. But I decided you wouldn't be inclined to read a chapter about morality, so I disguised it to make you think I would be regaling you with stories about trips to tropical locations. You're welcome.

Business travel draws out some very pertinent issues of faith, though. Travel is this weird exercise in which the one who travels is both alone and in a big group of people who are stressed and out of their familiar locale. Travel is an opportunity to both practice personal holiness and minister to others who could use a kind word or deed.

All Alone

The alone part is interesting because when I travel, I am mostly anonymous. In my hometown, I am well known for my generous nature and sophisticated wit (please allow me my fantasy). I see coworkers in the grocery store and customers at the auto repair shop. But when I travel, no one knows if I am a utility communicator or a dot-com billionaire, dressing in unfashionable clothes to be ironic, not because that's all I have in my closet. It's somewhat freeing to be unknown; I can let down my guard because there's a good chance I won't see these fellow travelers ever again.

That anonymity also creates the opportunity for me to behave badly. Not attacking-strangers-with-pool-noodles-badly but behaving even more selfishly and less disciplined than usual.

At home, I have a personal support structure to keep me on the straight and narrow. My actions, whether I am kind to others or mean to them, will get back to the people I know and about whom I care. I adhere to my personal standards not just because it's the right thing to do, but because I care what the people around me think of me. It acts as a bit of a behavior governor, helping to ensure I live up to a higher standard of conduct. That gives me extra motivation to put aside my selfish, carnal nature and act the way I want people to see me.

The structure of the familiar also helps me to do good things for my physical and spiritual health. I limit my screen time because others are aware of how much time I'm spending there. I sleep better because I am sleeping in my own bed. I eat better because we have a healthy family dinner. I have a better chance of exercising because I know the way to the Y and which cardio machines work. I am more consistent with my Bible study because my Bible and study materials are next to my favorite chair.

That support structure is missing when I travel alone. No one is monitoring what I watch, whether I exercise, how I treat other people. Of course, God is, and I'm accountable to him for how I act. And I would love to tell you that's all the motivation I need to be excellent every day. But without the added incentive of other people helping to keep me on the straight and narrow, I'm disappointed at how easily I slip away from my disciplined intentions.

All Together

While I'm all alone, I'm also generally in the midst of a great crowd of people who are also dealing with the stress of travel. We're usually not at our best in this situation. The world of work may sometimes feel like a rat race, but the stress and strain of business travel is a full-bore Rat Indy 500. This big group of people is one middle seat away from a meltdown. People are anxious, they are late, they are forgoing conveniences to try to save money, and they are tired. Just as I am anonymous in this crowd, so are they. It all adds up to people doing certain things I suspect they would not do at home. I have seen my fellow travelers yell at flight attendants, argue with other passengers about plane window shades, and storm away from the hotel desk because the hotel didn't have a king suite available that night.

I wish I could say I witnessed these things and immediately prayed prayers of blessings and comforted those who were distraught. But I generally don't. This great crowd of anxious, stressed people brings out my worst, too. In the midst of this giant group of stress, I tend to get even more impatient and entitled. When I think of the times I have not acted with God-given grace, nine times out of ten it has happened when I've been traveling.

I was on a recent flight surrounded by a family who was on their third of four legs of airline travel. Our plane had taken off late, and the family members were quickly realizing they would miss their connecting flight if the plane didn't land soon. The longer we circled the airport, and then waited for our gate after we landed, the more demonstrably anxious the mom got. Finally, she was in full meltdown and yelled a request that everyone allow the family to get out as soon as the door opened so they could make their next flight. I failed to pray for this family. Instead, I bristled at their anxiety and took it as my own. The experience left me feeling even more stressed.

That was silly because I had a two-hour layover before my next flight.

Responding Appropriately

Given the stress of travel, I need to recognize the need for some powerful preparation. I have to gird myself for a new environment where, if I'm not careful, I will minimize my faith and maximize my frustration.

My response is a collection of strategies to help me act on the road as I would like to think I act at home. I bring along uplifting reading materials and load spiritual message videos on my tablet so I have an alternative to less holy screen time. I bring a notebook and access to an online Bible study so I can maintain my morning habit. I pack exercise clothes and walking shoes so I have a better chance of getting some physical care while traveling. If I'm really preparing, I also invite Don, my accountability partner, to keep me in his prayers and quiz me when I get home so I'm accountable to someone while I am away.

The most important step toward remaining holy away from home, however, is to step back, take a deep breath, and pray for patience. I laughed out loud at God's wonderful provision recently when I found a prayer specifically for travel. David prays:

O LORD, you have examined my heart and know every-thing about me. You know when I sit down or stand up. You know my thoughts even when I'm far away. You see me when I travel and when I rest at home. You know every-thing I do. I can never escape from your Spirit! I can never get away from your presence! If I go up to heaven, you are there; if I go down to the grave, you are there. If I ride the wings of the morning, if I dwell by the farthest oceans, even there your hand will guide me, and your strength will support me. *(Psalm 139: 1–3, 7–10, NLT)*

Helping Others Through Their Stress

Finally, I need to stop focusing on my own stress and be atten-tive to how I can help others survive their stressful travel experi-ence. That can be as simple as helping someone lift a bag onto the rental car shuttle, offering to trade plane seats so a family can sit together, and expressing my deepest appreciation to the many staff people—from hotel clerks to shuttle drivers to flight attendants—whose job it is to keep me safe and make me comfortable away from home. My goal is to be able to say that I ministered in some way to at least one person on every business trip.

I'm sure that's what Jesus would have done. Although for me, it's harder, sitting in the middle airline seat, on a full flight, with a crying baby behind me and the man in front of me laying his seat back squarely into my lap.

But when I close my eyes, the Lobster Thermidor tastes divine.

Chapter 22:

True Repentance: Burning the Sorcery Scrolls

I'm just letting you know: This will be a short chapter.

It's short because it's about repentance, and I don't want to talk about that.

I don't want to talk about it, because the topic of repentance suggests that I have failed, and I don't like to admit that.

If it were up to me, I would just write, "Repentance is something we should all do if we want to clear the deck and seek God's forgiveness so we can go on our walk of faith without the distraction of sin holding us back. So, repent and get on with it."

And that would be the end of the chapter.

But apparently, I have more to say about this, because the chapter is still going on.

Repentance at Work

Repentance can feel especially out of place at work. If I say something unkind to my wife, I understand that I should repent and turn from doing that again. (If I don't understand that, she generally will remind me until I do.) But it feels even less natural to incorporate repentance at work. There's the fear of weakness in a competitive setting, the conflict with our pride, and the fact that we try to maintain a certain façade with our coworkers day in and day out. But that makes repentance even more important in the workplace. It's very hard to pretend I'm not a sinful creature, prone to gaffes, malicious intentions, and ugly behavior. Repenting of that has the potential to send a powerful signal to my colleagues that I accept responsibility for my bad behavior and want to change. When we put our egos on the line, we are telling others that we really do want to do better.

I've had plenty of repentance opportunities in my career. A major one occurred after I conveyed to colleagues something mean-spirited about a coworker. Not surprisingly, it got back to her, and she was very hurt. I stewed and struggled for a day. I considered pretending it didn't happen or that someone misheard or embellished what I said. But I knew that I had to repent and apologize. It was a very uncomfortable conversation, yet I knew I was doing the right thing. I don't believe she will ever see me as positively as I would like to be seen. But I also believe she recognized that I was truly sorry and committed to behaving better in the future.

More Than a Feeling

I think we get repentance wrong when we treat it as kind of a superficial response to our sin, like regret or sadness. I was drawn to a Sunday message our pastor gave recently. He said repentance is less a feeling and more a series of actions. It's a specific recognition of where we fell short, the act of renouncing what we did, reaching out to anyone who was wronged by our sin, potentially taking steps to make it up to that person in some way, and then committing whatever it takes not to do that again. There's a lot that goes into that version of repentance. And rightly so, given the importance God places on getting back on track when we fall off.

I still don't want to talk about it, though. I don't want to go down this path because underlying the need for repentance is the sense that I didn't live up to my expectations, let alone God's. My frail, fragile ego doesn't like that.

On top of that, going down the path of repentance means I need to make some acknowledgment of what I did. It's one thing to have a vague, general awareness of my sin. It's quite another to name it, own it, and acknowledge it. Potentially, I need to acknowledge it publicly, especially to someone harmed by what I did. My preference would be to pretend it didn't happen, hope no one finds out, and get on with things. Granted, when I do that, I am often convicted by a guilty conscience (and it's so much easier to attribute it to a "conscience," a nebulous passive sense of morality, rather than credit the active Holy Spirit jumping up and down until I deal with it). Often it feels easier to ignore that guilty conscience (or insistent Holy Spirit) rather than face facts.

Finally, if I'm really doing this repentance thing right, I need to change my behavior. Paul tells the Romans that the benefit of grace is not that we can go on sinning, but that we can turn away from our sin and be free from the death it brings (see Romans 5). However, that requires me to profess my sin and repent of it.

Consequences of Sin

The final challenge I have with repentance is that, by shining light on my sinful behavior, I am exposed to the consequences of that behavior. Here's where it really gets dicey, because the consequences can be significant. I think of David, repenting for counting his troops rather than trusting God for victory. David recognizes his sin and pleads with God.

> David was conscience-stricken after he had counted the fighting men, and he said to the LORD, "I have sinned greatly in what I have done. Now, LORD, I beg you, take away the guilt of your servant. I have done a very foolish thing." *(2 Samuel 24:10)*

Those of us who thank Jesus for the forgiveness of our sins may miss that taking away the guilt requires a response. In David's case, seventy thousand people died in a plague. Repentance opened the door for realignment with God, but that didn't remove consequences of the sin.

Change of Heart

True repentance means to turn from our behavior. We've all been recipients of namby-pamby apologies that weren't sincere and probably shouldn't have been said ("I'm sorry you think I did something wrong"). Or maybe you said them. They don't cut it. To truly repent means we need to change our hearts. We need to root out why we did wrong in the first place. It goes much deeper than the here and now. Once again, God is great at helping that transformation take place.

In my case, I had to do more than apologize for the cutting remark about my coworker. Seeing the pain I inflicted on a colleague forced me to do some deep soul-searching, since this was not the first time I had done something like that. I recognized that I needed to change my attitude so my speech would follow. If I didn't seek a deeper heart change, I would just continue to act and speak badly of others, and my apologies would be hollow and useless. I'm a long way from where I want to be. Like most aspects of my faith, I'm a work in progress. But I'm still seeking God's help to get better.

For a clear example of the action that should follow repentance, I love the story of the people of Ephesus when they were convicted of the truth of the new Christian movement they were experiencing. In response, they took a definitive step of repentance, helping to end the sinful behavior of their past lives. "Many of those who believed now came and openly confessed what they had done. A number who had practiced sorcery brought their scrolls together and burned them publicly" (Acts 19:18–19).

Sometimes we need to make a tangible sacrifice to demonstrate our commitment. Attitudes sometimes follow our actions. (My strong advice is that if you have sorcery scrolls that are guiding your career, it's probably best if you just go ahead and toss them into the fire.)

Finally, although we would like to think repentance is a one-and-done thing, it requires vigilance and perseverance to make sure we don't fall into old habits. Our pastor recommends continually re-rating our performance to be sure our hearts are oriented as they should be. He means that we should rate our performance against God's commands, not against others or our own sorry track record. Taking that step helps make sure that we're being attentive so the thing that tripped us up in the past doesn't trip us up again. (In my case, it means I can go on to find new things to trip me up.)

Lengthier Than I Intended

In conclusion, I seriously didn't expect this chapter to be this long. Apparently repentance is a topic I needed to process . . . for myself. You could have quit reading after the first four paragraphs. So, if you're still reading, then that's on you.

Because I don't need to repent for one more thing.

CHAPTER 23:

When It's Time to Go

I went to dinner recently with my friend John, a former colleague. I missed him very much since he'd left the company a few months previously. I had always enjoyed working with John because he had been a good friend, a trusted confidant, and someone who saw the world as I did. That, and he had a great sense of humor. Every conversation with John was guaranteed a minimum of 7.6 average laughs per minute (ALPM). I hadn't averaged more than 0.05 ALPM since he'd gone. (Not that I was spending all my time counting or anything.)

At dinner, I asked John about his decision to leave the company.

"Tell me, John," I said, with one hand in the pocket of my smoking jacket and the other holding my pipe aloft (not really, but it kind of adds to the atmosphere of the story). "When will I know that it's time for me to leave?"

"Oh," John said, leaning smartly on the fireplace mantle under the gaze of the mounted wildebeest head, twirling his waxed handlebar mustache (John's mustache, not the wildebeest's), "you'll know. Trust me, you'll know."

I've taken John at his word. I'm still at the same company, but I'm continually praying for God's guidance regarding if and when it's time to leave. These prayers fluctuate from not at all on days when things are going well to ferocious intensity on days when I feel there is no way I can come back tomorrow given the evil, the persecution, and the unmitigated fools I see everywhere I look. (Yes, I'm exaggerating once again. There's really not that much evil and persecution.)

Maybe I'm unique in this, but for those of us who follow Jesus and desire to follow him better, I think it's fairly common to question whether our current job is really what God wants us to do. As Christians in the business world, we wonder if we can really be effective in ministry when we're working in a secular environment. Doesn't doing ministry require that we work in a church, or at least at a nonprofit?

Of course, that's not the case. Our faith is not dependent on our external employment. In fact, many times our ministry is well-suited for a backstabbing, money-grubbing, ethics-deprived corporate workplace. If ever there was fertile ground for spreading the gospel, this is it!

But there are days when I struggle with how to proceed. The people are selfish, the boss is mean, and the clients are just plain wrong. I ask God, "If it's this hard, is this really where you want me to be? Is it time to move on?"

The Possibility of Moving On

We all leave our jobs at some point—sometimes by choice, sometimes not. Some of us find work we love and stay in the job for years before retiring, while colleagues fondly recall how we ministered to them. Some of us don't have that luxury, with employment cut short way too soon, leaving us to scramble to find something else to pay the bills. Some of us get fed up, throwing the laptop out a window and flipping over our desks as we storm out the door. (I'm praying my departure looks like the first, but I'm anticipating it will look more like the latter—with the added dynamics of security guards and television crews.)

You increase the likelihood of departures accompanied by law enforcement when your expectations are out of whack. When we expect guaranteed joyous lifetime employment, where coworkers and supervisors exude kindness and compassion and people line up outside our offices to hear the Good News about Jesus Christ, I think, just maybe, we're setting ourselves up for disappointment. If that's what we expect, it's no wonder things don't go our way.

That doesn't mean that God is far away in those instances. In some cases, the difficulties may be God's way of telling us to pick up and leave. In other cases, he may be telling us to stay put—he has more for us to do or he wants us to grow through this experience before it's time to move on. How do we know which is which?

Ill-Equipped to Decide

Deciding these kinds of major issues is difficult because we're human. Our emotions, egos, and finances cloud our decision making. We have a lot working against us.

For instance, the thought of leaving my current employment only crosses my mind on a bad day. When things are going well, in the back of my mind, I unconsciously expect that this current bliss will be the rest of my life, forever and ever, amen. I don't come home from a great day at work thinking, *Man, that was a really good day! I can't believe how much fun work was today! Is it time to get a new job?* Clearly, my attitude distorts my vision.

I'm also not a good judge of whether God desires me to change direction because my timing and God's timing often don't seem to align. I may be God's creation, but I can't figure why my clock and his clock don't track. When I want to move, he says, "Wait." When I'm comfortable and enjoying my rut, he says it's time to go. It's like God is on military time and I'm on metric. And since God's timing is always perfect, my metric watch is apparently due for repairs.

My clock and God's clock were off again the other day. Not surprisingly, it happened when I was having a bad day. I wanted to slam my security card on the boss's desk and tell her, in no uncertain terms, that I was currently contemplating exploring other opportunities for gainful employment in environments that might allow me to experience fresh growth opportunities and be more conducive to my overall well-being. And then I fantasized running down the hall screaming, "I'm free! I'm free!"

God, on the other hand, seemed to feel that engagement at my present employer might be good for me and my family and continue to offer an opportunity to shine a light on him for my coworkers' benefit. Once again, God (and a healthy dose of common sense) prevailed. My marathon through corporate hallways was postponed. (I go in on weekends just to practice, however. Eventually, the day will come.)

I had the opposite problem about a week later when a new volunteering opportunity showed up on my door. I didn't want a new opportunity. I had finally gotten my schedule into some form of non-chaos. I wasn't eager to take on any new commitments.

Nevertheless, I prayed about the opportunity—extremely conservatively and cautiously, lest I get an answer I didn't want. Despite my prayers pointed in the opposite direction, God gave me a clear sense that this was an opportunity I should pursue. It doesn't make the situation any better that it's been a rewarding and fascinating opportunity. I still pout while I'm involved in it.

Figuring It Out

Given how bad I am at rising above to resolve these important issues, I've been working to shore up my decision-making ability. A couple of techniques have produced good results.

First, I'm blessed to have a cohort of thoughtful, gifted, and spiritual friends who have provided wise counsel many times in my career. This group doesn't tell me the answer, despite my pleas for exactly that. They gently point me to Scripture, add me to their prayer lists, and share their experiences. They also remind me when I was a darn fool in the past and the way that turned out for me. It's a true blessing to have a group of friends and colleagues who are happy to shore up and sometimes counter my emotional responses. I have offered to provide the same support for them. Unfortunately, my counsel tends to sound something like "What happened to you is wrong! You should spray paint their office!"

I seldom get invited to offer my advice.

When I can take a deep breath, I eventually remember how powerful prayer and Scripture are in divining God's will for the situation. I say eventually because it usually takes me a long time to come to the stunning conclusion that I do not have the wherewithal to solve whatever challenge I'm facing, whether it's a malfunctioning copier or a company-wide layoff. Sometimes my prayers lead me to a sense of God's will, and sometimes they just help me come to terms with the situation.

Scriptural Direction

Second, Scripture can provide insight into how God has answered prayers like this before. When Jeremiah was ministering to the Israelites following the fall of Jerusalem, a group of army officers asked him to pray for direction for them. They were trying to decide if they should stay or go (sound familiar?). Jeremiah came back with a word from God telling people to stay in Babylon.

> He said to them, "This is what the LORD, the God of Israel, to whom you sent me to present your petition, says: 'If you stay in this land, I will build you up and not tear you down; I will plant you and not uproot you, for I have relented concerning the disaster I have inflicted on you.'" *(Jeremiah 42:9–10)*

If God can provide assurance that the Israelites will be fine in an enemy land, he can provide insight into whether I should stay put, too.

One of the most profound answers through Scripture came to me many years ago in a hotel room in Miami as I was on my way to a mission trip in Venezuela. I was heading to meet a group from another state, in a country where I wouldn't know anyone, at a time before cell phones. Frankly, I was terrified, and I prayed fervently to God about how I would navigate this strange land.

In an experience that still enthralls me, I did "Scripture roulette," randomly opening my Bible for guidance on how I could possibly do this, given that I was young, alone, and unable to speak the language. The first chapter of Jeremiah (Jeremiah again . . . coincidence?) seemed to be a specific assurance from God that I would be just fine.

But the LORD said to me, "Do not say, 'I am too young.' You must go to everyone I send you to and say whatever I command you. Do not be afraid of them, for I am with you and will rescue you," declares the LORD. Then the LORD reached out his hand and touched my mouth and said to me, "I have put my words in your mouth." *(Jeremiah 1:7-9)*

It was an incredible trip, one that still shapes my faith journey, dozens of years later.

I Read It in the Journal

There is another tool that has been a great blessing to help me discern spiritual direction. I've found that journaling is a powerful way to see where God has worked in my life and where I am supposed to go next.

If you're like me, you may not have thought much of journaling. I've always had some aversion to it. For one, it's a spiritual discipline, and those words alone repel me. Second, it feels like a lot of work. It takes time to step back from the crush of daily activities to write out my concerns, worries, prayers, and petitions. Third, I assumed journaling was only available to women. Part of it is the frilly spiritual journals they stock in Christian bookstores. Those journals tend to be pink and purple and have lots of cursive fonts that aren't easy to read. Those flamboyant books do more to turn men away from journaling than the "discipline" part. I bet if you sold a cracked leather-bound tool-belt journal, accessorized with tools that cut or make holes in things, men would out-journal women two to one.

Settling on the plain college-ruled paper approach, I discovered that journaling is a very intimate and revealing form of prayer. I find it to be like writing a daily letter to God. It allows me to slow down and think through the issues as I write them down. In the time it takes to write, the Holy Spirit can do some amazing work.

But I think the greatest benefit of a journal is that it allows me to see a trend in God's work in my life. By reading past journal entries with the benefit of knowing how the issue turns out, I see how God has answered prayers and created opportunities that blessed me. By connecting the dots of where God has led me up until now, I can get a greater sense of where God is leading me next.

A few weeks ago, at the end of a particularly brutal day, I thought my friend John was right; I knew it was time to go. After I had yelled at everyone in the house and slammed things down on the counter, I sat down with my journal and began reading. I had a different perspective on the struggles of the day when I saw the series of prayers God had answered in my life. The following day, I was wondering why I would ever think about leaving. It seemed clear that God was still working on me right here.

It's empowering to feel a sense of confidence that I am where God wants me to be. Those assurances remind me of the wonder of faith.

But I bet it would feel even better if I could drill some holes in things with my matching journal cordless drill/driver.

A Work in Progress

A fter years of trying, I have come to the startling conclusion that living out my faith at work is a challenge. It's hard to live out my faith in all aspects of my life. But it's at work where I spend most of my waking hours and where my faith performance gap seems most apparent. There are so many pitfalls, traps, and stumbling blocks to being both faithful and a good employee that I struggle to find the right balance.

If you doubt that, check out the twenty-three chapters that appear before this one.

Again, Paul's words captured it so well when he wrote to the Romans (apparently about me): "I do not understand what I do. For what I want to do I do not do, but what I hate I do" (Romans 7:15).

That's me. I do what I shouldn't and don't do what I should. I do:

- Make everything about me, even things that aren't remotely related to me
- Focus on the unimportant, elevating the petty things at work and minimizing the important things
- Apply an exhausting amount of effort to accomplish things in my own strength before I ever stop to consider where God fits in the equation

I don't:

- Invest enough in the people around me
- Thank God adequately for the blessings I've received
- Give God the room on the throne he deserves

All in all, I struggle with this. Despite years of practice, learning, reading, and sitting through sermons, I think any progress I might find would be measured in only fractions of an inch. There are days when I look back at my performance and feel I should probably just save myself from the embarrassment and give up.

Keeping On Keeping On

But I don't give up. I keep trying to better align my work and my faith because it's so important. When I get caught up in the daily work and only focus on the grind, I'm selling work short. Despite the daunting challenges of the workplace, work is a way of honoring the one who created us for work. Proverbs 16:3 calls us to "commit your works to the Lord" (NASB). Work is a form of worship, a field of mission, and an opportunity to use the talents God has given us. It's a golden opportunity to see God's hand at work if we only pay attention. Knowing how personal our God is, I try hard every day to be attentive lest I miss a miracle in my presence, sometimes for my benefit.

Despite my missteps and setbacks, I keep trying to live out my faith at work. I fall short (a lot), mostly because I get in my own way. Or I think I can successfully blend work and faith if I just work harder. But I find that I make progress if I focus on the right things.

I focus on God's plan. Although my approach to personal improvement usually entails applying more effort, I know I need to be engaged in a way that isn't dependent on my own strength. To internalize that, I spend time reading the Bible, reading Christian authors, watching Christian videos, hearing Christian messages, and drawing near to wise Christian friends. I am slowly, tentatively, finding ways to surrender to God's authority and control. Each step forward encourages me to keep at it.

I focus on people. In the intensity of a workday, the daily work tasks may seem the most pressing. But it's the people who matter. When I'm at work, I try to focus on the people around me, since that's what God cares about.

I focus on the important things. I am so easily distracted by the petty, inconsequential, and fleeting elements of work. But Paul calls us to keep a clear focus on what is upright so we can experience God's peace, even at work.

> Finally, brothers and sisters, whatever is true, whatever is noble, whatever is right, whatever is pure, whatever is lovely, whatever is admirable—if anything is excellent or praiseworthy—think about such things. Whatever you have learned or received or heard from me, or seen in me—put it into practice. And the God of peace will be with you. *(Philippians 4:8–9)*

I embrace the grace I am given, knowing that I am God's work in progress. Life on earth is short and requires intentional focus if we are to notice sufficient growth during that time. When I immerse my life in Christ, I grow in the right way. "And as we live in God, our love grows more perfect" (1 John 4:17, NLT). I know that God is still working on me, and that motivates me to keep trying to do what God asks of me in the relationship, "being confident of this, that he who began a good work in you will carry it on to completion until the day of Christ Jesus" (Philippians 1:6). I am a work in progress.

An Issue of Trust

At the end of the day, beating myself up for my own poor performance is another manifestation of my own pride and desire for control. I generally have to forcibly pull myself out of the driver's seat. (This is often a challenge, since not being in the driver's seat means I don't get to decide where we're going. Nor do I get to decide the internal temperature or what radio station is playing.) When I look at what happens when I do trust God, I'm typically amazed. Because God is faithful.

The longer I have been in the workforce, the more time I have had to see God's hand at work. So many things that threatened to overwhelm me in the moment have fallen away over time. Situations change. Crises dissipate. Coworkers and bosses who made me angry have retired or moved on. One particularly frustrating boss, who pelted me with constant nagging and criticism of my work, is now living on a farm raising chickens. (I understand those chickens are miserable under her continued nagging and criticisms.) The situations that seemed interminable at the time ended or changed and turned out just fine. The more I've recognized that, the more I've grown in my ability to get through the temporary tough time to see what God was doing in my life. And he was—and is—doing good things. Praise God!

Sharing the Good News

My purpose in writing this book was to share my experience in the hopes that it would encourage you. (OK, my real purpose in writing this is to use up the old typing paper that I've had since college. But if that helps you, too, great.)

Every day I work alongside, and hear about, fellow Christians who also struggle to find a way to live fully in their faith while fully at work. I hear stories like mine of how people and policies at work don't live up to our expectations for a holy workplace, and we struggle to respond. My hope in sharing my journey is that it encourages you, too. I hope now that you know how poorly I navigate these issues, you recognize that your progress is superior to mine. I hope it encourages you to keep on traveling. We're all in this together, and we all share the same power and promises provided by a loving and gracious God.

Taking the Next Step

So, I keep at it. In the process, I delight to experience God's double helpings of mercy and grace. I'm encouraged to keep trying, keep learning, keep applying what I know. When I'm open to them, I see miracles every day.

I also keep trying even though I don't know where the journey will lead. As professor and author Dallas Willard said, we don't need to know the whole path, just the next step. Willard reportedly answered a question about where someone should start if they wanted to grow spiritually. His response was simple and certainly feels true: "Do the next right thing you know you ought to do."

I hope his response is encouraging to you, too. But at the very least, at the end of this book, now you know (in obnoxious detail) there is someone out there who also struggles with the challenge of navigating faith and work. If nothing else, you can celebrate that you're not the worst Christian at work.

I think we would all benefit from a simple goal: Be like Jesus. But if you can't be like Jesus, at least be better than Tom.

ACKNOWLEDGMENTS

Don't let anyone fool you: Writing a book is the easy part. Remembering everyone who deserves your heartfelt thanks, well, that's where it gets overwhelming.

It's easy to start with Cathy, who has been my best friend, as well as a kind, generous, and gracious partner, through more than 147 years of marriage. Thank you, my love, for all you pour into me every day.

Thank you, too, to Ellen and Christian, who every day teach me so much about life and passion, wit, and love. Since I'm your father, I think I'm supposed to be teaching you, but I will soak it in, nonetheless.

Thank you, Mom, for giving me a love of reading and writing, and my brother, Craig, for reminding me I've wanted to write a book since I was a kid.

Thank you to Don Ferris, who has been my long-time accountability partner—or, as we prefer to call it, "acceptability partner."

But let's get to the book part. I have to start with the team from Morgan James Publishing, with a tip o' the proverbial cap to Terry Whalin, who made it easy to take my vision and turn it into this thing you're holding. Thank you, Terry, for chasing me down and tackling me to sign the publishing agreement!

I'm incredibly grateful to Amanda Rooker of Split Seed Media for being much more than an editor. Amanda guided, counseled, and coached me. She also ripped into poorly written copy with frightening ferocity, yet at the same time using a gentle touch and kind words. If any of the concepts in this book make sense, you can thank Amanda for looking out for you, dear reader.

While I'm at it, I need to give a shout-out to Lin Johnson and her tireless work on the Write to Publish conference. It's so otherworldly to think I have been attending WTP for almost twenty years—with a big, what, sixteen-year gap in the middle? I always say Write to Publish is where I know I will meet (and sometimes wrestle with) God, and it happens every time I go. Thanks for your stewardship of this precious event for so many years, Lin.

It was nerve-wracking to think of someone other than me reading what I wrote, so I started with a cabal of like-minded people to get their feedback and insight. Thank you to my "editorial board": Scott Drzycimski, Luke McCoy, Jennifer Schuchmann, Marlon Vogt, and Troy Weary. I am so grateful for your willingness to beta-test this thing. I'm sure the side effects won't last, and you'll go on to lead normal lives very soon.

I have to give special thanks to Jennifer Schuchmann. I am exceedingly grateful for the opportunity to rekindle a friendship with someone I so admire, respect, and just plain enjoy. Thank you, Jennifer, for not holding back, for calling out manuscript malfeasance when you see it. You make me laugh every time we talk, and I'm looking forward to building on our friendship when I'm not blatantly using your wisdom for my personal gain.

I owe my employer a big ol' pile of thanks, too. I know corporations are supposed to be heartless, soulless beasts, but ITC, you are truly something special. Thank you to the colleagues with whom I've worked over the years, culminating with the Marketing and Communications team and my own boss, Krista Tanner. You have been the recipient of so many of the obnoxious behaviors I spelled out in this book. Yet you have given me far more grace than I deserve (which is kind of the definition of grace, I guess.) Thank you. I miss you.

It's also important that I thank the pastors who have provided me with such a strong biblical foundation over the years. Thank you, Jack Quandt, Ron Connerly, Steve Packer, John Seitz, Greg Johnson, and now Jason Ishmael at Antioch Christian Church (www.LifeIsForLiving.org). You might not have known it, but as you spoke, I was furiously soaking it in, taking copious notes, and stealing your words to make up a book that I could sell to other people. I'm so glad you are all pastors, since that would make it kind of awkward for you to sue me for plagiarism. Thanks for sharing the good stuff!

Finally, and this may feel a little weird, but I do owe an enormous debt to God, Jesus, and the Holy Spirit. Even if no person ever reads this book, the past year has been such an intimate, deep, and exhilarating spiritual journey. My new counsel to people is to take on a project that is entirely dependent on God's provision, and he will meet you there. If this book hits the remainders pile on the day it is released, that's perfectly fine. Because the intensity with which I have pursued God in writing this is totally worth it. And it's probably exactly the kind of activity that makes God happy.

Thank you, friends. I am humbled and grateful. And I am blessed to be blessed by this journey.

About the Author

Tom Petersen is a husband, father, son, and long-time utility communications guy, with two master's degrees and a deep and bitter jealousy of anyone who has a PhD. He has been a church elder, nonprofit board member, and homeowners' association board president, which is just about the worst job in  the entire world. He has lived his entire life in one state in the Upper Midwest but has traveled to at least three other states, so he considers himself quite sophisticated and worldly. He is rude, self-centered, and unpleasant, but he thinks a lot of serious and important things are very funny. The fact that he continues to take up space on this planet is clear testimony to the gracious hand of a loving God.

For more information, please visit
www.tomcpetersen.com

ENDNOTES

1   Os Hillman, "Today God Is First: Working versus Striving," May 24, 2023, Today God Is First, https://todaygodisfirst.com/working-versus-striving/.

2   Os Hillman, "Today God Is First: Failure Leads to Godliness," January 5, 2023, Today God Is First, https://todaygodisfirst.com/failure-that-leads-to-godliness/.

3   Mark D. Roberts, "Caring Leadership," October 5, 2022, Life for Leaders, Fuller De Pree Center, https://depree.org/caring-leadership/.

4   Peggy Noonan, *The Time of Our Lives: Politics, Passions, and Provocations* (New York: Hachette, 2017), 94.

5   Os Hillman, "Today God Is First: When Insecurity Turns Evil," October 16, 2023, Today God Is First, https://todaygodisfirst.com/when-insecurity-turns-evil/.

6   Mark Roberts, "The High Calling: Finding Freedom From Worry," Theology of Work, https://www.theologyofwork.org/the-high-calling/daily-reflection/finding-freedom-worry.

A free ebook edition is available with the purchase of this book.

To claim your free ebook edition:

1. Visit MorganJamesBOGO.com
2. Sign your name CLEARLY in the space
3. Complete the form and submit a photo of the entire copyright page
4. You or your friend can download the ebook to your preferred device

A **FREE** ebook edition is available for you or a friend with the purchase of this print book.

CLEARLY SIGN YOUR NAME ABOVE

Instructions to claim your free ebook edition:
1. Visit MorganJamesBOGO.com
2. Sign your name CLEARLY in the space above
3. Complete the form and submit a photo of this entire page
4. You or your friend can download the ebook to your preferred device

Print & Digital Together Forever.

Snap a photo

Free ebook

Read anywhere